BATTLEFIELD WALKS:
Northumbria &
The Scottish Borders

Brian Conduit

Published by Sigma Leisure – an imprint of
Sigma Press, 5 Alton Road, Wilmslow, Cheshire SK9 5DY, England.

British Library Cataloguing in Publication Data
A CIP record for this book is available from the British Library.

ISBN: 1 85058 825 2

Typesetting and Design by: Sigma Press, Wilmslow, Cheshire.

Cover photograph: Roman re-enactment, Chesters Fort, Hadrian's Wall.
© Graeme Peacock, www.graeme-peacock.com

Maps: Bute Cartographics. Reproduced from Ordnance Survey mapping on behalf of The Controller of Her Majesty's Stationery Office. © Crown Copyright. Licence Number MC 100032058

Printed by: Progress Press Ltd, Malta

Disclaimer: the information in this book is given in good faith and is believed to be correct at the time of publication. No responsibility is accepted by either the author or publisher for errors or omissions, or for any loss or injury howsoever caused. Only you can judge your own fitness, competence and experience. Do not rely solely on sketch maps for navigation: we strongly recommend the use of appropriate Ordnance Survey (or equivalent) maps.

Preface

There is no piece of country in Britain that has been more fought over or contains more physical evidence of past conflicts than the quiet border country between England and Scotland. Centuries of warfare extend from the Roman period – and probably earlier – to the middle of the 18th century when the defeat of Bonnie Prince Charlie's forces at the Battle of Culloden in 1746 finally brought peace and stability to the area.

Walking battlefield sites is a pleasurable experience and, given the popularity of recent television series on this subject, appears to be one that is growing in popularity.

The following selection contains a few urban or semi-urban routes but most are rural walks in thinly-populated countryside. As well as providing the obvious benefits of walking activities in general – fresh air and physical exercise – these walks arouse historical interest and stimulate the imagination. And it has to be said that at times a great deal of imagination is required as there is often little to see on the ground and it is difficult to envisage the site at the time of the battle. The main problem is that battlefields are not protected in the same way as ancient buildings and historic monuments. At the time of the battles most were used for agricultural purposes and this has continued. In more recent times some of them have been built on by housing or industrial premises and have modern road and railways running across them. Some are inaccessible because there are no public rights of way across them, although in all cases the sites can be viewed from adjacent roads, lanes and footpaths. Only a few have well-signed 'Battle Trails' with information boards. The nearest that they have to any protection is that some of the more important and historic battlefields are registered and their owners, and other interested parties, are given advice on ways to conserve and enhance these sites and to encourage greater public access.

Despite these limitations and a certain degree of frustration at times, there is much to be enjoyed in overlooking and walking across these battlefields. We can try to visualise them at the time of the conflict, working out the positions and strategies of the opposing armies and imagining the scenes of carnage, suffering, brutality, bravery, terror and heroism. Many of the battles played a vital role in our history, particularly in the relationship between the two historic nations of England and Scotland.

Most of the sites are in peaceful and tranquil surroundings and situated amidst attractive and in many cases spectacular countryside. Some have features of interest nearby – perhaps a ruined castle, old church, abbey or Roman site – to add to the interest and enjoyment of the walk.

The battlefield walks are supplemented by routes featuring other military events in the area. These include the first recorded Viking raid on these shores, on the Holy Island of Lindisfarne in 793; two of the many sieges of the two greatest border strongholds, Carlisle and Berwick-upon-Tweed; the fates of abbeys, on both sides of the border, that were caught up in the incessant warfare; and, in more recent times, a surprise attack by the German navy on the east coast of England at the start of World War I. Above all no guide to battlefield and other military walks in this part of the country can omit the grandest military monument in the whole of Britain, Hadrian's Wall.

Where relevant, suggestions for possible follow-up visits to sites in the locality – not on the actual route – that have a link with the battle have been included. These may be a museum that has displays and exhibits to do with the event or a memorial in a local church connected with those who were involved in the battle. All of these help to build up a picture of those stirring, violent but memorable events that took place in the past but have helped to shape the present.

Brian Conduit

Contents

Introduction   1
    The Border – a Battle Zone   1
    Anglo-Scottish Wars   1
    Physical Evidence of Conflicts   3
    Uncertainties and disagreements   4
    Further reading   4

The Walks

1   Defence of Roman Britain: Hadrian's Wall, 2nd to 5th centuries   6
    Distance: 5 miles (8km)
    Time: 3 hours

2   Viking attack on Lindisfarne, 793   12
    Distance: 4 miles (6.4km)
    Time: 2 hours

3   Edward I at Lanercost Priory, September 1306 to March 1307   17
    Distance: 4½ miles (7.2km)
    Time: 2½ hours

4   Great Siege of Berwick, May to July 1333   22
    Distance: 3 miles (4.8km)
    Time: 1½ hours

5   Battle of Halidon Hill, 19 July 1333   27
    Distance: 2½ miles (4km)
    Time: 1½ hours

6   Battle of Neville's Cross, 17 October 1346   31
    Distance: 5½ miles (8.9km)
    Time: 3 hours

7   Battle of Otterburn, 19 August 1388   37
    Distance: 3 miles (4.8km)
    Time: 1½ hours

8   Battle of Homildon Hill, 14 September 1402   41
    Distance: 6 miles (9.7km)
    Time: 3 hours

9 Battle of Hedgeley Moor, 25 April 1464   46
> **Distance:** 2½ miles (4km)
> **Time:** 1 hour

10 Battle of Hexham, 15 May 1464   50
> **Distance:** 6 miles (9.7km)
> **Time:** 3 hours

11 Battle of Flodden, 9 September 1513   55
> **Distance:** 7 miles (11.3km)
> **Time:** 3½ hours

12 Battle of Solway Moss, 24 November 1542   61
> **Distance:** 5 miles (8km)
> **Time:** 2 hours

13 Destruction of Kelso Abbey and Roxburgh Castle, 1540s   66
> **Distance:** 4 miles (6.4km)
> **Time:** 2 hours

14 Battle of Ancrum Moor, 27 February 1545   71
> **Distance:** 3 miles (4.8km)
> **Time:** 1½ hours

15 Battle of Pinkie, 10 September 1547   76
> **Distance:** 6 miles (9.7km)
> **Time:** 3 hours

16 Battle of Newburn Ford, 28 August 1640   81
> **Distance:** 6½ miles (10.5km)
> **Time:** 3 hours

17 Battle of Philiphaugh, 13 September 1645   86
> **Distance:** 6½ miles (10.5km)
> **Time:** 3½ hours

18 Battle of Dunbar, 3 September 1650   91
> **Distance:** 4 miles (6.4km)
> **Time:** 2 hours

19 Battle of Prestonpans, 21 September 1745   96
> **Distance:** 3 miles (4.8km)
> **Time:** 1½ hours

20 Bonnie Prince Charlie at Carlisle, 1745   101
> **Distance:** 2½ miles (4km)
> **Time:** 1½ hours

21 Battle of Clifton Moor, 18 December 1745   106
Distance: 4 miles (6.4km)
Time: 2 hours

22 German raid on Hartlepool, 16 December 1914   110
Distance: 3 miles (4.8km)
Time: 1½ hours

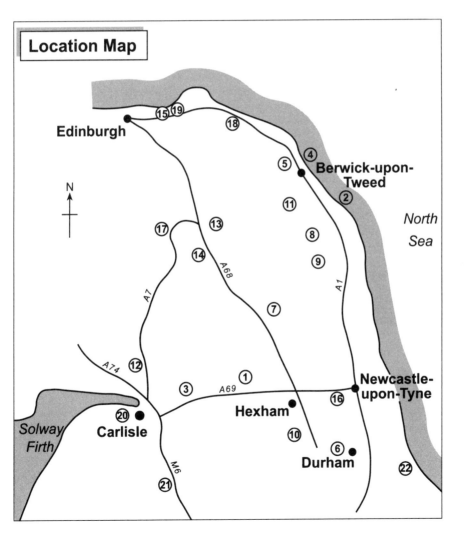

Introduction

The Border – a Battle Zone

For centuries the border area between England and Scotland was the bloodiest and the most fought over land in Britain. Therefore, it is hardly surprising that there are battlefields and other physical evidence of conflict in abundance. Warfare between England and Scotland was almost continuous, especially between the late 13th and the middle of the 16th century and did not finally end until the defeat of Bonnie Prince Charlie at the Battle of Culloden in 1746.

Of the 22 walks in this guide, 17 are directly concerned with Anglo-Scottish warfare. The other five include Roman military control of Britain, Viking raids, two battles in the Wars of the Roses and a German raid on an east coast port in World War I.

Anglo-Scottish Wars

Why was there so much warfare between England and Scotland and why was the Border Country so unsettled for such a long period?

Basically, the kings of England had always had some vague claim to be overlords of the whole island of Britain and, at various times, Welsh princes and Scottish kings were happy to accept this as long as they were left alone within their own territories. In addition, there were inevitable territorial disputes between England and Scotland over the so-called 'Debatable Lands' around the Solway and other areas near the border. For centuries, the line of the border was constantly being altered and strategic border strongholds, particularly Carlisle, Berwick-upon-Tweed and the now-vanished town of Roxburgh, changed hands many times between the two kingdoms.

A long period of relatively good relations between England and Scotland ended with two events towards the end of the 13th century: the accession of Edward I to the English throne in 1272 and the death of Alexander III of Scotland in 1286. The new English king, strong-willed and warlike, was determined to assert this vague claim of his predecessors to have overlordship over Britain more actively. First he conquered Wales, encircling it with powerful fortresses, and then the death of the Scottish king gave him an opportunity to intervene in the affairs of the Scottish crown in the 1290s.

The heir to Alexander III was his granddaughter Margaret, 'the maid of Norway', who was living in Scandinavia at the time of her accession to the Scottish throne. Unfortunately she died in 1290 while on her journey to Scotland and this plunged the country into a succession crisis. As overlord, Edward I acted as adjudicator between the various claimants and chose John Balliol, largely because he was likely to be little more than an English puppet ruler. This provoked a nationalist backlash in Scotland, led first by William Wallace and later by Robert Bruce. Wallace's revolt was brutally suppressed but after the death of Edward I in 1307 and the accession of his far less warlike and decisive son, the Scots were successful in clearing the English out of Scotland. In 1314, Robert Bruce inflicted a most humiliating defeat on Edward II and the English army at Bannockburn.

The recognition of Scottish independence by the Treaty of Northampton in 1328 did not end the conflict. In the reign of Edward III, far more like his grandfather than his weak father, the English retaliated and centuries of warfare followed. Even when the two kingdoms were technically at peace there was irregular warfare between the various landowners on both sides of the border. These powerful landowners, largely independent of royal control from either London or Edinburgh, were able to do much as they pleased in the remote and warlike borderlands. One of the greatest and long running feuds was that between the Percy family (English) and the Douglas family (Scottish) and members of those families figure prominently in many of the battles.

The Anglo-Scottish wars spilled over into continental affairs. France was traditionally Scotland's ally against England and the 'Auld Alliance', as it was called, posed an almost constant threat to English kings. It left their northern frontier, their back door, vulnerable while campaigning against the French in continental Europe and gave them both a motive and a pretext for intervening in Scottish affairs. For Scottish kings the alliance with France was a vital form of security against their more powerful southern neighbour.

Several events occurred in the 16th and 17th centuries that eventually brought peace between the two British nations. The Protestant Reformation created a religious bond between them and a corresponding rift between aggressively Protestant Scotland and Catholic France. As a result of a marriage alliance arranged by Henry VII, the crowns became united in 1603 when James VI of Scotland inherited the English throne on the death of Elizabeth I and became James I of England. A century later the countries themselves were united when the Act of Union created the United Kingdom of Great Britain in 1707.

Even so there were still the two Jacobite rebellions of 1715 and 1745 and it was only after the defeat of Bonnie Prince Charlie at Culloden in 1746 that warfare was finally over. Culloden proved to be the last battle ever fought on British soil.

Physical Evidence of Conflicts

What impact have these centuries of warfare had on the landscape of Northumbria and the Scottish Borders? For a start there is Hadrian's Wall, the grandest Roman monument in Britain, which represents the first attempt to draw some kind of dividing line to separate the northern and southern halves of this island.

Both sides of the border are littered with the ruins of the great castles built to defend settlements and territories on both sides of the border. As well as the large castles, there are many minor ones, such as pele towers (mini-castles) and bastles (fortified farmsteads). At Corbridge in Northumberland, situated on the River Tyne and possessing some impressive Roman remains, even the vicarage was fortified. Inevitably, elaborate defences sprang up around the main towns of the area – Newcastle, Carlisle, Berwick and Durham.

Durham was the centre of power of the prince bishops, responsible to the monarch for the protection of England's northern frontier. One of the most exciting and impressive visual experiences in this island is to gaze up at the mighty cathedral and castle at Durham. The former was memorably described by Sir Walter Scott as 'half church of God, half castle 'gainst the Scot', and towers above the steep, wooded banks of the River Wear. These adjacent buildings are the twin symbols of the authority of the medieval bishops of Durham and illustrate this power more vividly than any words.

Durham Cathedral suffered several attacks from the Scots and the remains, some of them fairly meagre, of the many abbeys on both sides of the border – Lanercost, Melrose, Dryburgh, Kelso, Jedburgh – are a reminder that religious institutions, far from being oases of peace and tranquillity, were often in the thick of the fighting, bloodshed and violent politics of the area.

Berwick-upon-Tweed is the classic border town. Throughout the Middle Ages, it changed hands 14 times between England and Scotland, only finally becoming English in 1482. Here you can admire and walk around the 16th-century fortifications, the most advanced in this country and among the finest in Europe, immensely expensive and state of the art at the time. Elizabeth I had them built because of her concern for the security of her northern border. They were never used because the death of the queen, the last purely English monarch, in 1603 led to the accession of James VI of Scotland as James I of England. But these walls stand as a reminder of centuries of bloody strife between the two nations, a strife that forms the bulk of this battlefield-walking guide.

The battle of Flodden (1513) was one of the bloodiest of the many Anglo-Scottish conflicts. A simple inscription on the monument that stands on the battlefield sums it all up: 'to the brave of both nations'.

Uncertainties and disagreements

When walking battlefield sites, it is important to be aware that a lot of the information about battles and battlefields is conjectural and open to question and debate. A lack of detailed, accurate and especially unbiased historical evidence means that, in the case of many battles, the interpretation of that evidence is an area of conflict, especially amongst specialist military historians. Therefore, disagreements do arise regarding the exact site and events of the battle and the precise disposition of rival armies.

Further reading

A.H. Burne – *The Battlefields of England* (Penguin, 2002)

John Kinross – *Discovering Battlefields of England and Scotland* (Shire, 1998)

David Smurthwaite – *The Complete Guide to the Battlefields of Britain* (Michael Joseph, 1993)

Philip Warner – *British Battlefields* (Cassell, 2002)

Ken and Denise Guest – *British Battles* (Harper Collins, 1996)

Neil Fairbairn – *A Traveller's Guide to the Battlefields of Britain* (Evans, 1983)

1

Defence of Roman Britain: Hadrian's Wall, 2nd to 5th centuries

The first and last parts of the walk are along the Hadrian's Wall Path National Trail either side of Housesteads Fort. The middle stretch is along a path which runs along the base of the wall. This enables you to appreciate the wall from the point of view of both the defenders and potential attackers. The all-round views are magnificent, stretching from the northern Pennines and South Tyne valley to the Border Forests.

Start: Housesteads Fort, grid ref NY794684

Distance: 5 miles (8km)

Time: 3 hours

Parking: Housesteads

Refreshments: Kiosk serving drinks and snacks at Housesteads

Map: OS Explorer OL 43 (Hadrian's Wall)

Hadrian's Wall

There are no specific battles or known major military encounters between the Romans and their attackers but the wall itself was potentially a constant battle zone. In fact, the whole area around it was a military zone.

Hadrian's Wall was more than just a wall; it was a highly sophisticated military complex of which the wall was only one – if the main – component. Emperor Hadrian ordered its construction around AD122 because he was alarmed at the state of disorder in the area. Its purposes were to mark and regulate the northern frontier of the

Housesteads Fort from the South Gate

Roman province of Britain and to act as a base both against attacks. It was a defence from the Caledonian tribes to the north, outside the empire, and against possible rebellions amongst the tribes to the south.

The wall runs across the narrowest part of northern England from the Solway Firth to the mouth of the River Tyne and is 73 miles long. The best preserved and most spectacular section is the middle part, running either side of Housesteads. Little survives in the east, which is now mostly covered by the houses of Newcastle and surrounding towns or by the 18th-century military road, partly constructed on top of it. The western (Cumbrian) section was rifled to provide building stone for many of the local farms. When complete the wall was about 15 feet high, with a parapet of around 6 feet on top of that, and was between 8 to 10 feet wide. On the north side was a V-shaped ditch, except where the wall runs on top of steep cliffs making additional defence unnecessary, and on the south was a broad, flat-bottomed ditch called the vallum. This is thought to have indicated the boundary of the military zone around the wall, separating it from the civilian zone to the south.

Along the length of the wall 17 forts were built and between them, approximately at intervals of a mile, were a series of mini-forts or milecastles. Between the milecastles were turrets, which were lookout posts. A road called the Military Way ran between the wall and vallum linking the forts and a series of back up and supply forts lay a few miles to the south along an earlier road called the Stanegate. There were certain recognised official crossing points of the wall, mostly at the forts and milecastles.

The soldiers who built the wall were legionaries; these were Roman citizens and the elite of the Roman army. Those who subsequently manned it were auxiliaries, troops recruited from the various parts of the empire.

Despite the elaborate nature of the wall, it was breached and overrun on a number of occasions and was continually being altered and partially rebuilt. For example the western part was originally constructed from turf but was later rebuilt in stone. The wall was temporarily abandoned by the Romans when they pushed further north and built a turf wall, the Antonine Wall, across the central lowlands of Scotland, but they later returned to Hadrian's Wall to make it a permanent frontier of the empire. It was finally abandoned in the early 5th century when the Romans withdrew their legions from Britain.

The Route

1. Go through a kissing gate beyond the National Trust shop and information centre onto a path which winds up, via another gate, to the fort. Where the path bends left to the museum, keep ahead uphill across grass beside the west wall of the fort.

   Housesteads is generally regarded as the finest and best-preserved of all the forts on or close to Hadrian's Wall. It has the usual playing card shape, common to most forts throughout the empire, and contains foundations of the headquarters building (the administrative centre of the fort), the commandant's house, barracks, granaries and latrines. It is well worth exploring the fort and visiting the adjacent museum.

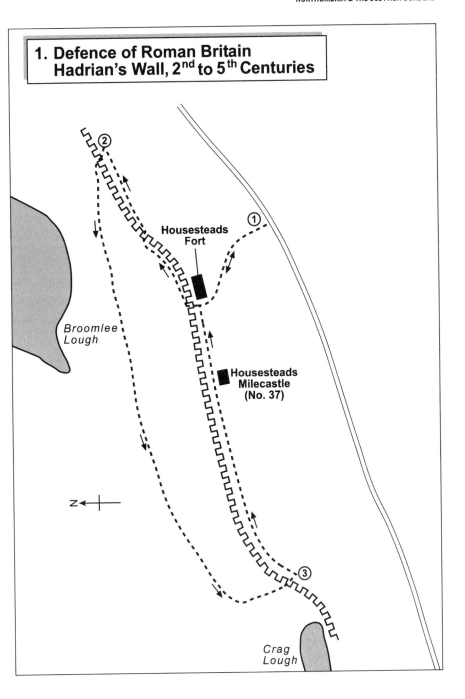

1. Defence of Roman Britain
Hadrian's Wall, 2nd to 5th Centuries

Housesteads Fort

Housesteads Milecastle (No. 37)

Broomlee Lough

Crag Lough

Bear left to a gate and go through it onto the Hadrian's Wall Path. Turn right, immediately descend steps and walk beside the wall, which here forms the north wall of the fort. At the corner of the fort, the wall descends into a dip where you go through a gate. This is Knag Burn Gateway, a rare example of a gateway that is not at either a fort or milecastle. It was created in the 4th century, possibly to relieve the pressure on the busy fort of Housesteads.

After going through it, head uphill, now with the wall on the left. Climb a stone stile, keep ahead through a small area of woodland, climb a ladder stile and continue on a switchback route beside the wall.

2. In a dip – just before the wall ascends to Sewingshields Crags – turn left over a ladder stile and follow a path across rough, boggy grassland towards a conifer plantation. Climb a stile on the edge of the plantation, continue through the trees, climb another stile on the far side and continue along a clear grassy path, with the wall on the left and Broomlee Lough on the right.

Soon after climbing another ladder stile – this is where the route crosses the Pennine Way – you keep by the right edge of a plantation and continue to reach a track at a waymarked post. Turn left, climb a ladder stile, continue along the track towards a farm, go through a gate, pass to the left of the farm buildings and keep ahead to a stone stile.

3. After climbing it you rejoin the Hadrian's Wall Path and immediately turn left over a ladder stile. Now follows a spectacular, energetic, 'up and down' walk beside the wall back to Housesteads, arguably the finest remaining section of Hadrian's Wall. The all-round views are magnificent and the wall is continuous. After about three-quarters of a mile (1.2km) you reach milecastle 37, one of the best preserved on the wall. As you can see, it is a miniature version of Housesteads, with a gateway in the wall and neat barrack blocks.

Walk around its perimeter, continue by the wall, go through a gate and walk through a belt of trees. Housesteads is just beyond the trees and after turning right through a gate, you rejoin the outward route and head downhill back to the car park.

What else is there to see?

There is a Roman Army Museum near Greenhead a few miles to the west of Housesteads Fort

2

Viking attack on Lindisfarne, 793

The walk starts in the small village at the south end of the island and the main historic sites – priory, church, museums and castle – are all located at this end. On the circuit of the island, you pass close to these sites, walk by rocky shores and sand dunes and enjoy superb views across to the mainland, the latter dominated by the imposing bulk of Bamburgh Castle.

Note that Holy Island is connected to the Northumberland mainland by a causeway that is covered at certain times of the day. Always consult the tide tables before crossing, either by the roadside at the start of the crossing or by phoning Berwick TIC (01289 330733)

Start: Holy Island, car park at north end of village, grid ref NU127420

Distance: 4 miles (6.4km)

Time: 2 hours

Parking: Holy Island car park

Refreshments: Pubs and cafés at Holy Island

Map: OS Explorer 340 (Holy Island & Bamburgh)

Lindisfarne 793

During the 7th and 8th centuries, after the long period of chaos and confusion that followed the withdrawal of the Romans from Britain and the invasions of the Angles, Saxons and Jutes, England developed into a collection of seven kingdoms. The most important and powerful of these were Northumbria in the north, Mercia in the

Lindisfarne Priory: built by the Normans on the probable site of the Anglo-Saxon monastery sacked by the Vikings

Midlands and Wessex in the south. The kingdom of Northumbria was noted for its art and scholarship, especially prolific in the great coastal monasteries. From the monastic centres of Jarrow and Wearmouth, the Venerable Bede, 'Father of English History', produced his *History of the English Church and People.* On the isolated island monastery of Lindisfarne, opposite the royal Northumbrian stronghold of Bamburgh, the beautiful manuscript of the Lindisfarne Gospels, a masterpiece of Anglo-Saxon art, was created in the 690s.

A monk called Aidan founded the monastery on Lindisfarne in 635. He did this at the invitation of King Oswald of Northumbria and, from there, he spread Christianity throughout the kingdom. As well as being a centre of missionary activity, the monastery on Lindisfarne became noted for its scholarship and craftsmanship. One of its most famous monks was St Cuthbert and it was to honour his memory that the Lindisfarne Gospels were produced.

In 793, a terrible and unexpected event occurred that was to destroy this scholarship and bring Northumbria to its knees. The

Anglo-Saxon Chronicle vividly describes it in these words. "In this year terrible portents appeared over Northumbria which sorely affrighted the inhabitants: there were exceptional flashes of lightning, and fiery dragons were seen flying through the air. A great famine followed hard upon these signs; and a little later in that same year, on the 8 June, the harrying of the heathen miserably destroyed God's church on Lindisfarne by rapine and slaughter."

The Chronicle is describing the Viking attack on Lindisfarne. There may well have been earlier attacks on undefended coastal monasteries but this was the first recorded attack by Viking seafarers on the coasts of Britain. As such, it is regarded as the start of the Viking Age, the beginning of over two centuries of destruction, conquest, trade and settlement involving the nations of the British Isles and the fledgling kingdoms of Scandinavia.

An even more graphic account is provided by Simeon of Durham. "And they came to the church of Lindisfarne, laid everything waste with grievous plundering, tramped the holy places with polluted feet, dug up the altars and seized all the treasures of the holy church. They killed some of the brothers; some they took away with them in fetters; many they drove out, naked and loaded with insults; and some they drowned in the sea."

Viking attacks on Lindisfarne and on many other exposed and therefore vulnerable coastal monasteries continued but eventually the monks decided that enough was enough. They abandoned the island in 875 and moved to the mainland in search of greater security, carrying with them the body of St Cuthbert.

The Route

1. Turn right out of the car park and at a T-junction, turn left, in the Priory direction. At the next T-junction, turn right and immediately left to enter a grassy square. In order to visit the priory, church and museum, keep ahead but to continue with the route, bear left diagonally across the square to the Crown and Anchor Inn.

    Nothing is left of the original Anglo-Saxon monastery burnt and pillaged by the Vikings in 793 and over the following years. The

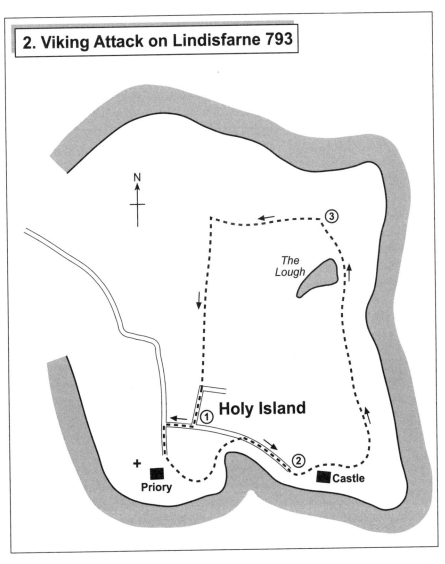

2. Viking Attack on Lindisfarne 793

present ruins are of a later foundation; a Benedictine priory established by the Normans in 1082 and thought to occupy the same
site. It was dissolved by Henry VIII in 1536. The nearby parish
church of Holy Island, as Lindisfarne was later known, was built
in 1122.

After making your way across to the Crown and Anchor, turn right in front of the pub entrance to a turnstile and public footpath sign. Go through, walk across a field and go through another turnstile on the far side. Turn left, keep beside the shore to a T-junction and turn right along a lane towards the castle. There were no fortifications on Holy Island until the 16th century, when the first defences were constructed by Henry VIII. The small castle was built in the reign of Edward VI as a protection against Scottish raids. After falling into ruin, it was restored in the early 20th century and handed over to the National Trust in 1944.

2. At a fork immediately beyond a kissing gate, take the left-hand path which passes below the castle walls. Go under a footbridge and bear left to continue either at the base of a low ridge or along the top of it to a gate. There are wonderful sea views from here and it may well have been along this stretch of coast that the Vikings landed in 793. Go through the gate, keep ahead to go through another one and soon the small lake called The Lough is seen on the left.

3. After the next gate you enter an English Nature National Nature Reserve. Turn left along a path, initially by a wall on the left, and follow it across rough grassland near the base of dunes to a footpath post. Turn left along a broad, straight, grassy track. The track later becomes a lane, which leads back to the start.

What else is there to see?

There is much on the history of the Holy Island of Lindisfarne, including the Viking attacks, both in the Priory Museum and the Lindisfarne Heritage Centre. The latter also houses an exhibition of the Lindisfarne Gospels; the originals are in the British Library.

3

Edward I at Lanercost Priory, September 1306 to March 1307

As well as passing the impressive ruins of Lanercost Priory, the walk includes two fragments of Hadrian's Wall, part of which formed the northern boundary of the lands of the medieval priory. There are also extensive views over the Irthing valley and across the Solway to the Southern Uplands and the hills of Galloway, and an attractive walk beside the River Irthing.

Start: Banks East Turret, grid ref NY575647

Distance: 4½ miles (7.2km)

Time: 2½ hours

Parking: Banks East Turret

Refreshments: Hotel at Lanercost

Map: OS Explorer 315 (Carlisle)

Lanercost Priory, 1306-1307

Given its location near the Scottish border, the priory of Lanercost was permanently in a no-win position. For around three centuries it was in the middle of a war zone and was either bankrupted by having to host kings of England or destroyed during raids launched by kings of Scotland. During a reign of 35 years, Edward I, the 'Hammer of the Scots', visited Lanercost on three occasions – 1280, 1300 and 1306 – and the priory was attacked by William Wallace and Robert Bruce – in 1296, 1297 and 1315 – and again by David II in 1346.

Edward I's last visit in 1306 was his most memorable. By now, he

Lanercost Priory, effectively the seat of the English government during the winter of 1306-07

was an old man of 67 and this was to be his final attempt to conquer Scotland. His stay at Lanercost was meant to be a short one but he fell ill while there and he and his vast entourage – over 200 – had to spend the winter at the priory. In all he stayed for over six months and, apart from greatly inconveniencing the running of the priory, this lengthy stay considerably depleted its financial resources, especially as the king contributed virtually no money.

Lanercost Priory effectively became Edward's campaign head-quarters during the winter of 1306-1307 where he planned what he hoped would be his final and successful conquest of Scotland. Throughout this period the priory became a small town and, in order to house the king and his followers, a huge wooden building, basically a temporary royal palace, had to be constructed. It is thought that this was probably built on the land between the outer gatehouse and the west front of the church. Temporary stone structures were erected as well.

Edward I finally left Lanercost in March 1307 but he did not have long to live. Shortly afterwards he died while crossing the Solway, leaving an undefeated and revengeful Scotland that was to inflict a humiliating defeat on his son seven years later at Bannockburn.

The Route

1. Facing the superb view over the Irthing valley, turn right to Banks East Turret. A turret was a watchtower and this is one of the best-preserved on Hadrian's Wall. It was built of stone and incorporated into the original turf wall in this Cumbrian section of the wall. The turf was later replaced by stone.

   Immediately beyond the turret, a stone stile leads onto an enclosed path, which runs parallel to the road. Another stile returns you to the road and you head downhill through the hamlet of Banks. At a fork, take the right-hand lane to a T-junction, turn left and at a Hadrian's Wall Path sign to Walton, turn right along an enclosed track which heads uphill to a fragment of the wall at Hare Hill. Although only a fragment, it is significant as one of the tallest remaining parts of the wall. The stretch of wall around here marked the northern boundary of the estates of Lanercost Priory.

   A little further on, where the track turns right, turn left and walk along the right edge of a field, passing in front of a farmhouse. Go through a gate and continue along a track by the right edge of a succession of fields and via a series of gates and stiles. Eventually you descend to a kissing gate to the left of a farm. Go through, cross a track, go through another kissing gate and keep ahead along an enclosed path. After the next kissing gate, continue steadily downhill and at the bottom corner of the field, go through another kissing gate.

2. Turn left along a tarmac track. The track keeps along the right edge of Abbey Gills Wood, curving first left and later curving right to reach a road at Lanercost. Keep ahead – in the Brampton direction – to the priory entrance.

   Stones from nearby Hadrian's Wall were used in the construction of Lanercost Priory, founded as an Augustinian priory in 1166 and dissolved by Henry VIII in the 1530s. Its nave is still in use as a parish church and the ruins of the east end are particularly complete and impressive and a fine example of early Gothic architecture. The area between the gateway and the church is considered

3. Edward I at Lanercost Priory 1306-1307

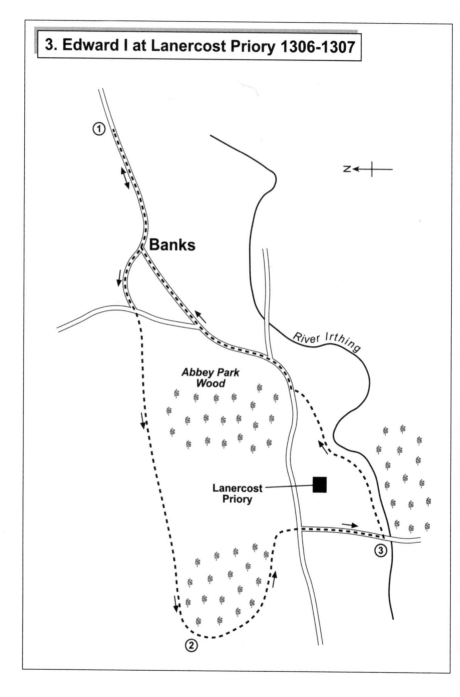

the most likely site for the temporary wooden palace that was erected by Edward I during his stay here throughout the winter of 1306-07. The English Heritage commentary, available to visitors to the priory, provides details on that momentous and lengthy royal visit.

Continue along the road towards Lanercost Bridge.

3. Just before reaching the bridge and the Abbey Bridge Hotel, turn left through a kissing gate, at a public footpath sign to Island Cottages. Now comes an attractive stroll by the tree-lined River Irthing, with fine views of Lanercost Priory across the meadows on the left. The path later bears left away from the river to continue along the right field edge to a kissing gate.

Go through and turn right along the road that curves left uphill into Banks. On reaching a Hadrian's Wall Path sign, you rejoin the outward route and retrace your steps to the start.

4

Great Siege of Berwick, May to July 1333

The walk basically comprises a circuit of Berwick's unique fortifications, with an extension along the banks of the river, passing the three famous and contrasting bridges over the Tweed, to the scanty remains of Berwick Castle. Frequent rebuilding and updating of the town and its defences mean that little survives from the 1333 siege. But this is a fascinating walk that tells you much about the violent history of this area and the views – across the river, over the town and along the coast – are outstanding.

Start: Berwick-upon-Tweed, in front of the Town Hall, grid ref NT999528

Distance: 3 miles (4.8km)

Time: 1½ hours

Parking: Car parks in Berwick-upon-Tweed

Refreshments: Pubs, cafés and restaurants in Berwick-upon-Tweed

Map: OS Explorer 346 (Berwick-upon-Tweed) or town map of Berwick

The Siege

Berwick-upon-Tweed has seen many sieges throughout its history and the town changed hands between England and Scotland more than any other in the country – 14 times – until finally remaining English in 1482. The Great Siege of 1333 was one of the longest, lasting three months.

After Robert the Bruce's decisive victory over Edward II of England

The scanty remains of Berwick Castle are virtually the only visual reminder of the 1333 siege

at Bannockburn in 1314, Scottish independence was safe for the time being and was officially recognised by Edward III at the Treaty of Northampton in 1328. However, with the death of Robert the Bruce in 1329, the familiar problems reappeared. His successor, David II was only 5 years old and Edward Balliol, son of John Balliol, an English puppet who had ruled Scotland during the 1290s, returned from exile with an army. He was crowned king in 1332 but was soon ousted by Sir Archibald Douglas and the Earl of Moray. Balliol withdrew to the Borders where he sought help from Edward III. Naturally, the English king was only too delighted to assist.

In March 1333, Balliol laid siege to Berwick which, at that time, was in Scottish hands. After about two months, Edward III and an English army joined him and in May the siege of Berwick began in earnest. Among the techniques used by the besiegers was an early form of biological warfare that comprised catapulting the severed heads of dead soldiers into the town in order to cause disease.

After nearly two months, Berwick's defences were crumbling and both besiegers and defenders were becoming frustrated. Eventually an agreement was made that there would be a truce and that if Berwick was not relieved within 15 days – by 11th July – the town would surrender to the English. This truce was guaranteed by 12 hostages and among these were the two young sons of Sir Alexander Seton, the deputy commander of the town. Scottish hopes depended on the arrival of reinforcements led by Sir Archibald Douglas. Douglas managed to send some supplies into the town but Edward III did not consider this sufficient to qualify as relieving it. In order to lure the besiegers away, Douglas then threatened to march south and pillage northern England.

Edward called his bluff. Gallows were erected as close to the walls of Berwick as possible and some of the hostages, including the two young boys, were hanged. A new and somewhat confusing agreement followed; there would be a further truce until 20 July and Berwick would surrender to the English if not relieved by then. The failure of Douglas to draw the English king away from Berwick by attacking Bamburgh and his crushing defeat at the Battle of Halidon Hill on 19 July sealed the town's fate. On the following day, Berwick surrendered to the two Edwards, Edward III of England and Edward Balliol, the latter soon to be reinstated as King of Scotland.

The Route

1. Start in front of the 18th-century Town Hall, walk up Marygate and in front of Scotsgate, turn right up steps and continue along Greenside Avenue. Turn left up more steps and turn right along the top of the Elizabethan walls. These enclose a smaller area than Berwick's original medieval walls and were constructed around the north and east sides of the town between 1558 and 1570. They are unique to Britain and repay careful attention, constructed to an advanced design to withstand artillery power. Although prohibitively expensive, Elizabeth I, constantly in fear of attack from the continent, considered them essential for the defence of her vulnerable northern frontier. The accession of James VI of Scotland as James I of England on the queen's death in 1603 and the subsequent reduction in warfare between England and Scotland rendered them obsolete and they were never put to the test.

4. Great Siege of Berwick 1333

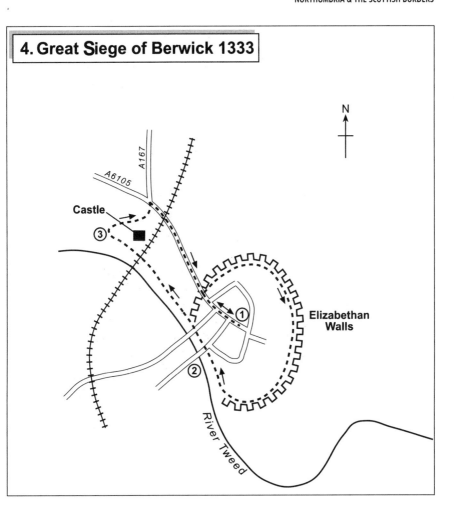

Follow the ramparts around the north and east sides of the town, passing the impressive Cumberland, Brass and Windmill Bastions which clearly illustrate the advanced design and murderous gunfire potential of these ramparts. On the wall walk, you pass close to Holy Trinity church, built between 1650 and 1652 and one of only two churches in England built during the Cromwellian period, and the early 18th-century barracks. After passing King's Mount, you descend from the walls and continue by the River Tweed along the south side of Berwick. The Elizabethan defences did not extend along the river and the medieval defences survive here, though they are known as the Georgian walls as they were largely rebuilt in the 18th century.

2. After crossing a road on the north side of the Old Bridge, built in the early 17th century in the reign of James VI and I, keep ahead first along Bridge Terrace and then along a tarmac riverside path. The Elizabethan walls start again over to the right but your route continues beside the river, passing first under the Royal Tweed Bridge (1928) and Robert Stephenson's towering Royal Border Bridge, built to carry the main east coast railway line between London and Edinburgh and opened in 1850. Just beyond this great viaduct are the remains of Berwick Castle.

This was one of the greatest of border fortresses and was the main target of the English army in the Great Siege of 1333. The castle later fell into disrepair and the construction of the Elizabethan defences in the 1560s rendered it largely obsolete. The final blow came when Robert Stephenson drove the railway literally through the middle of it and built Berwick station largely on the site of the great hall in which Edward I had adjudicated on the question of the Scottish succession in the 1290s. Little is left of the medieval castle, apart from the west wall which reaches down to the river, but its significance is that it is one of the few structures in Berwick that date back to the siege of 1333.

3. About 100 yards (91m) beyond the castle remains, turn sharp right onto another tarmac path which ascends alongside the castle to a gate. Go through, continue winding uphill and go through another gate onto a road. Turn right, cross the railway bridge by Berwick station and keep ahead along Castlegate. After passing under Scotsgate, retrace your steps to the start.

5

Battle of Halidon Hill, 19 July 1333

Several conservation paths have been created across Halidon Hill to form battlefield trails and this route follows one of them. It takes you across the heart of the battle site and the extensive panoramic views, especially over Berwick and the Tweed estuary, clearly reveal the military advantages of the English army's hilltop location.

Start: Halidon Hill Battle Site, signposted from A6105 1½ miles (2.4km) north west of Berwick-upon-Tweed, grid ref NT981546

Distance: 2½ miles (4km)

Time: 1½ hours

Parking: Halidon Hill Battle Site

Refreshments: None

Map: OS Explorer 346 (Berwick-upon-Tweed)

The Battle

The Battle of Halidon Hill arose out of the Great Siege of Berwick and was a Scottish attempt to relieve the town by defeating the besieging English army. Edward III of England was besieging Berwick as part of his plan to assist Edward Balliol to regain the Scottish throne. A pliant puppet king of Scotland, friendly to England and hostile to France, would be very much to the advantage of the English king.

During the course of this long siege – three months – a truce was arranged that unless the town was relieved by 20 July, it would surrender to the English army. A Scottish army, led by Sir Archibald Douglas, tried to draw the English army away from Berwick by marching south into England and attacking Bamburgh but this tactic was unsuccessful. Douglas returned to Scotland, camped at Duns and on the morning of 19 July marched to Berwick. This was the last day on which he could relieve the town before the truce ran out.

Meanwhile Edward III and the English army moved a short distance to the north and established themselves in a strong position on top of Halidon Hill. Although the English had the better position, the Scots had the larger numbers as the English army had been weakened by desertions. Edward divided his army into three divisions: he commanded the centre, Sir Edward Bohun led the right wing and Edward Balliol led the left wing. The Scots were also organised into three divisions, led by the Earl of Moray, Robert the Steward and Sir Archibald Douglas.

As the Scots advanced across the very marshy ground at the base of the hill, their horses became bogged down, the cavalry troops had to dismount and they became sitting targets for the English and Welsh archers. Wave after wave of arrows descended on the slow moving Scottish soldiers and the subsequent English cavalry charge swept them from the field of battle and led to wholesale slaughter. One of the casualties was Douglas himself.

It was a crushing defeat for the Scots but for Edward III it was sweet revenge for his father's humiliating defeat at Bannockburn. Berwick duly surrendered to the English, Edward Balliol was reinstated as king of Scotland and David II went into exile in France. As an English puppet ruler, Balliol did his master's bidding and ceded Scottish territory to England, which hardly endeared him to his subjects. David II was to return later, seeking revenge.

The Route

1. There is an information board and viewfinder in the car park. From here, the views extend over Berwick and the Tweed estuary, along the Berwickshire coast and inland to the line of the Cheviots and the distinctive three peaks of the Eildon Hills on the horizon. The view indicates how vulnerable Berwick was to an assault by the English army.

    Turn left out of the car park along the lane and take the first track

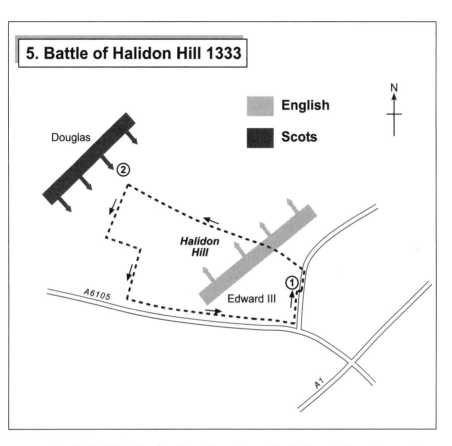

5. Battle of Halidon Hill 1333

English

Scots

N

Douglas

②

Halidon
Hill

A6105

Edward III

①

A1

on the left. This hedge-lined track, called Grand Loaning, takes you across the heart of the battlefield. The English occupied the hilltop and the Scots were drawn up on the lower ground to the north. Information boards indicate the English position.

2. After three-quarters of a mile (1.2km), look out for where a Conservation Walks waymark directs you to turn left over a stile and head steadily uphill along the right edge of a field. In the top corner, turn left to continue along the right edge, turning first right and then left to pass the trig point on top of Halidon Hill, 535 feet (163m) high and another superb viewpoint. Just before the next field corner, turn right over a stile and head downhill along the right field edge.

Looking over Berwick-upon-Tweed from the Battle of Halidon Hill. The battle was an attempt to lift the siege of the town in 1333.

Turn left in the bottom corner to continue along the right edge of a succession of fields and over a series of stiles, parallel to the A6105. Finally turn left, head uphill – still along the right field edge – and climb a stile in the top corner onto a lane. Keep ahead to return to the start.

6

Battle of Neville's Cross, 17 October 1346

It requires a great feat of imagination to appreciate or understand the battlefield of Neville's Cross today as much of it is covered by roads and suburban housing on the western edge of Durham. In fact, the main vantage point is a pedestrian crossing over a busy dual carriageway. Despite these disadvantages, this is a most attractive and rewarding walk. Some parts of the battle site remain as woodland and green fields, especially those parts occupied by the Scottish army. In addition, the historic city of Durham, with its striking castle and cathedral and lovely riverside woods, provides a superbly attractive introduction and conclusion to the walk.

Start: Durham, Market Place, grid ref NZ274425

Distance: 5½ miles (8.9km)

Time: 3 hours

Parking: Plenty of car parks in Durham

Refreshments: Pubs, cafés and restaurants in Durham

Map: OS Explorer 308 (Durham & Sunderland)

The Battle

Despite the English victory at Halidon Hill, the unpopular Edward Balliol, regarded by most Scots as an English puppet king, was driven into exile and David II returned to Scotland in 1341. By now Edward III was heavily engaged in the Hundred Years' War with France and in 1346 the English army inflicted a crushing defeat on the French at Crecy. In the same year, David II invaded northern

Durham Cathedral and Castle above the River Wear, within sight and sound of the Battle of Neville's Cross

England, partly for revenge but mainly in response to a request for assistance from his French ally, Philip VI.

The Scottish army marched on Durham and camped in the Bearpark, an estate belonging to the priors of Durham just to the west of the city. Meanwhile, in the absence of both Edward III and the Prince Bishop of Durham in France, the Archbishop of York, together with Ralph Neville and Henry Percy, hastily gathered together an English army at Bishop Auckland.

As they advanced on Durham, the English vanguard surprised and routed a Scottish raiding party, led by Douglas, which fled over Sunderland Bridge to inform their colleagues of the proximity of the English army. The two armies met at Neville's Cross, 1 mile (1.6km) to the west of Durham, named after an ancient preaching cross. It is alleged that after the battle, Ralph Neville – the names are purely coincidental – had a new cross erected in commemoration of the victory.

The English army assembled on the ridge of Red Hill and the Scots lined up a little to the north on Crossgate Moor. To the east was the steep wooded ravine of Flass Vale – then a bog – and to the west the valley of the River Browney. The Scots had a tremendous numerical advantage; they had around 16,000 men while the English, severely depleted because of the war in France, could scarcely muster 5,000. But as the Scots advanced across the moor towards their opponents, they were repeatedly mown down by the English archers. Wave after wave of attacks was halted with heavy losses, although the Scottish spearmen, commanded by Robert Stewart, fought skilfully and did cause some confusion to the English right wing. A series of successful charges by the English cavalry eventually won the day. The Scots were pushed back and those that remained on the field of battle were encircled. It was during the final stages of the battle that David II was wounded and captured.

As they tried to escape the carnage, the Scottish soldiers were hampered by the terrain, either drowned as they swam across the River Browney or slowed down as they tried to cross Flass Bog. After his crushing defeat and capture, the Scottish king spent the next 11 years in captivity in England. He was released and restored to the Scottish throne in 1357 following the payment of a ransom of £66,000.

The Route

1. Start in the Market Place and walk up Saddler Street, signposted to Cathedral and Castle. At a fork, continue along the right-hand street, which is lined by attractive old buildings, now mostly used by Durham University, and follow it past the castle and the east end of the cathedral. Go under an arch – the site of a gateway in the medieval walls of the city – and cross Prebends Bridge over the River Wear. From here, there is a memorable view of Durham Cathedral and the adjacent castle, twin symbols of the power of the medieval prince bishops, rising majestically above the river. The mighty cathedral, built mainly between 1093 and 1133, is regarded as a masterpiece of Norman architecture. Although much altered and rebuilt, especially in the 19th century when it became part of the new university, Durham Castle retains the plan of the original Norman stronghold of the bishops.

Turn right and, at a fork immediately ahead, take the left-hand upper path through woodland and go up steps onto a road. Cross over, take the road opposite and keep ahead on joining a major road. At a public footpath sign just after a right bend, bear left, pass beside a gate and head quite steeply uphill along a tarmac path to emerge onto a road. Keep ahead into Neville's Cross.

2. Just before reaching the remains of the old cross – only the base has survived – turn right along St John's Road and where it ends, turn left along a tarmac path to the A617. Turn right alongside the road, cross a railway bridge and then cross the footbridge over the road. An information board on the bridge points out the details of the battle, the site of which lies to the north on Crossgate Moor, now largely obliterated by the railway line, main road and suburban housing. The English position was immediately in front of you.

After crossing the road, turn back towards the railway bridge and turn right along Quarry House Lane. The lane peters out into a track and you follow it around left and right bends. By the gate to Quarry House Farm, bear left onto a path, which descends through trees to a stile. Climb it and keep ahead along the bottom edge of sloping woodland. The path continues beside the River Browney to reach a lane to the right of a bridge.

Many Scots were drowned in this small river as they tried to escape after the defeat of their army. Turn right up to a road.

3. Turn right again and at a public bridleway sign, turn left along an uphill tarmac track. Pass between farm buildings, go through a gate, walk along a left field edge and go through another gate. The fields to the right – one of the few remnants of the former Crossgate Moor not built upon – are where David II and the Scottish army drew up at the start of the battle.

Walk across the next two fields and on the far side of the second one, turn right – ignoring the stile in the field corner to the left – and continue along the left edge of the field. Keep along the left edge of a series of fields but look out for where you turn left over a

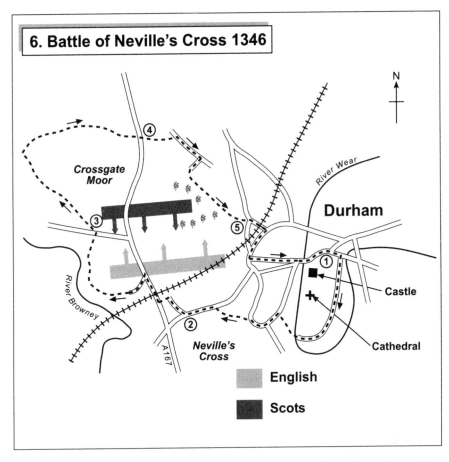

6. Battle of Neville's Cross 1346

stile. Walk along an enclosed path, which bends right and continues to a road.

4. Cross carefully – this is a very busy road – and take the enclosed tarmac path opposite which emerges onto a road. Keep ahead, take the first road on the right and turn right again into Larches Road. Where the road ends, keep ahead along an enclosed path to a T-junction and turn left along the left edge of a steeply-sided, wooded valley. This is Flass Vale, formerly a treacherously boggy area which greatly hampered some of the Scottish soldiers while trying to escape after the battle. Descend steps, curving right, turn

right on joining another path and at a crossways, turn left. Follow an undulating path through the trees to reach a road.

5. Keep ahead towards the railway viaduct and at a T-junction, turn right, passing under the viaduct. Bear right uphill, turn left into Allergate and bear left steeply downhill along Crossgate to cross Framwelgate Bridge over the Wear. Continue uphill along Silver Street to return to the Market Place.

7

Battle of Otterburn, 19 August 1388

The first and last parts of the walk involve short stretches beside the A696. On the middle section, you enjoy extensive and striking views over the open landscape of Redesdale on a gradual climb along a track and across rough pasture which takes you across the heart of the battlefield. This is followed by a descent along a quiet, narrow lane. In such empty terrain, the battlefield can have changed little in the last 700 years.

Start: Otterburn Battle Site car park, on A696 three-quarters of a mile (1.2km) west of Otterburn village, grid ref NY876935

Distance: 3 miles (4.8km)

Time: 1½ hours

Parking: Otterburn Battle Site

Refreshments: Pubs and cafés at Otterburn

Map: OS Explorer OL42 (Kielder Water & Forest)

The Battle

The battle of Otterburn was one of the classic conflicts in the long feud between two of the most powerful of the Border families, the Percies on the English side and the Douglases on the Scottish side.

Taking advantage of the fact that the English king Richard II was a minor, James Earl of Douglas led a raiding party into England in 1388. The Scots reached Durham, which they burned and pillaged, but were held by an English army led by the Percies – Henry (nicknamed Hotspur) and his brother Ralph – in a skirmish outside Newcastle. During the skirmish, Douglas captured Hotspur's lance pennon, his personal flag, and allegedly taunted him to recover it. For medieval

Overlooking the battlefield of Otterburn from Percy's Cross

knights this was regarded as a grave matter of honour and it was a challenge that Hotspur could not disregard. Douglas left to return to Scotland, with the Percies in pursuit, and on his way back made an attempt to capture Otterburn Castle in Redesdale.

Douglas set up camp just to the west at Otterburn and waited for the Percies, thus virtually issuing an open invitation to Hotspur to attempt to recover his pennon. The English army arrived there in the evening of 19 August and Hotspur decided to surprise the Scots with a night attack. It was a risky strategy. The English army was inevitably tired after a long march while the Scots had been resting in camp for most of the day. In addition, the feared English archers, whose deadly longbow attacks were often the main reason for victory against the Scots, would be largely ineffective in night fighting.

Hotspur planned a two-pronged assault. While he advanced on Douglas's men from the front, Sir Thomas Umfraville was sent on an outflanking manoeuvre to the east and north of the Scots to attack them from the rear. The strategy did not work. The Scots took the initiative and, superbly led by Douglas, charged at the main English army. The fighting was fierce but the Scots were successful and both Hotspur and Ralph Percy were captured. Even the death of Douglas during the confused hand-to-hand fighting did not weaken Scottish resolve as the Earl of Dunbar proved to be a more than adequate replacement. By morning, the battle was over and the Scots had gained a decisive victory.

Umfraville, who had taken virtually no part in the conflict, led the defeated English army back to Newcastle and the Scots, led by Dunbar, returned over the border. The Percies were later released.

The Route

1. The Percy Cross, which stands in the car park sheltered by trees, is not actually a cross but a standing stone resting on a plinth. It was erected in 1777 as a monument to the Percies and to mark the site of the battle. There are two information boards, one of which over-looks the battlefield.

    Leave the car park and turn left along the road – there is a footpath all the way – into Otterburn. Take the first road on the left but a lit-tle further along the main road is the site of the now-vanished cas-tle, on the east bank of the Otter Burn and now occupied by a hotel. After turning left, head gently uphill. It was roughly along the line of this road that Umfraville marched on his unsuccessful mission to surprise the Scots from the rear. Nowadays – appropri-ately perhaps – it leads to Otterburn Army Camp.

2. At a public bridleway sign, turn left along a track to a gate. Go through, walk between farm buildings and continue along the track, at first with a wall on the left and later with a wall on the right, passing through three more gates. This is the heart of the battlefield. Looking over the valley, the English were to the left near the village and castle, while Douglas and the Scottish army occupied the higher ground to the right near the hamlet of Greenchesters.

    After the third gate, continue steadily uphill across open, path-less, rough pasture, making for a group of thinly-spaced trees on the ridge in front and looking out for another gate. Go through the gate and keep ahead – the going is rougher now as you have to pick your way between the stumps and branches of a felled conifer

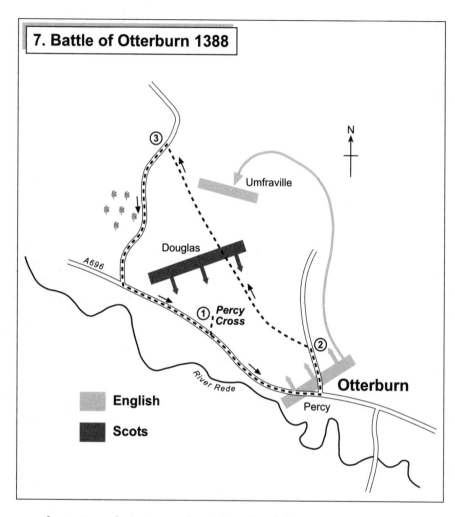

7. Battle of Otterburn 1388

Umfraville

N

A696

Douglas

① Percy Cross

② Otterburn

River Rede

English

Scots

Percy

plantation – keeping to the right side of the scattered trees to reach a narrow lane.

3. You should reach the lane where a footpath post points in the direction you have just come. But it does not really matter as, wherever you hit it, you turn left and follow the narrow, twisting lane downhill through the hamlet of Greenchesters to the A696. Turn left to return to the start – at first you have to walk along verges but later a footpath appears.

8

Battle of Homildon Hill, 14 September 1402

Homildon Hill lies just to the west of Wooler and public footpaths lead out of the town to the site of the battle, giving you fine views over the battlefield and enabling you to walk across a good part of it. This is quite an energetic walk with plenty of climbing but well worth the effort for the stunning views of the Cheviots, Tweed valley, Northumberland coast and the Scottish border country. Just to confuse you, the name Homildon Hill does not appear on Ordnance Survey maps as it is now called Humbleton Hill

Start: Wooler, Market Place at bottom end of High Street, grid ref NT992280

Distance: 6 miles (9.7km)

Time: 3 hours

Parking: Wooler

Refreshments: Pubs and cafés at Wooler

Map: OS Explorer OL16 (The Cheviot Hills)

The Battle

In 1399 Henry of Bolingbroke deposed Richard II, who was later murdered, and became Henry IV, the first of the Lancastrian kings. Having acquired the throne in such dubious circumstances, his chances of retaining it were somewhat precarious and by 1402 he was facing serious challenges. There was a major revolt in Wales led by Owen Glyndwr, the traditional ties between Scotland and France

The Scots were lured from their strong position on Homildon Hill and suffered a heavy defeat

were becoming closer, and Archibald, Earl of Douglas was rampaging through Northumberland with a Scottish army.

Like Otterburn fourteen years earlier, the Battle of Homildon Hill was another in the long history of conflict between the Percies and Douglases. While the king dealt with the Welsh revolt, it was left to Sir Henry Percy, Earl of Northumberland, and his son Hotspur to confront the Scots. After reaching as far south as the Tyne and attacking Newcastle, Douglas turned back towards the borders but the Percies outflanked him and barred his way near Wooler. Having received advance warning of the English position, Douglas wisely deployed his men on Homildon Hill – now called Humbleton Hill – and waited for the English to attack.

Percy ordered his archers onto the adjacent Harehope Hill and from there they led a sustained and highly effective assault on the Scots, spreading terror in their ranks. This had the effect of luring them from their strong hilltop position and as they charged in desperation down the slopes, the English archers followed them and continued their deadly fire. Once on the flatter land of Red Riggs Field, where the bulk of the English army was deployed, the depleted Scots were further cut down by the English cavalry and they fled in large numbers from the field of battle. Some managed to reach as far as the Tweed, only to be drowned while attempting to swim across the river

It was a striking victory for the Percies. Not only had their old enemy Douglas been defeated but he was also captured in the battle. However, their triumph was soured by the king who, breaking with the usual custom, demanded that Douglas and the other Scottish prisoners should be handed over to him. This was regarded as an insult by the Percies who refused. The outcome was that in the following year the Percies, becoming increasingly disenchanted with Henry IV over the question of financial compensation and other matters, allied with the Welsh rebels and marched southwards. In the ensuing Battle of Shrewsbury, the king was victorious and Hotspur was killed.

The Route

1. From the Market Place turn up Ramsey's Lane, signposted St Cuthbert's Way, and after almost half a mile (0.8km), bear left, at a public bridleway sign, onto an uphill track to a gate. Go through, turn right across to another gate and turn left along a path. At a junction about 50 yards (46m) ahead, take the right-hand uphill path, which bends left and heads more steeply uphill.

   At a fork, continue along the right-hand path across open grassland towards conifers and, at the next fork, take the left-hand path and go through a gate to enter the plantation. Continue uphill through the trees and at a fork – soon after reaching the top – take the left-hand path which descends to a gate. Go through – here leaving the conifers – and at a fork immediately ahead, take the left-hand path across open grassland to reach a waymarked post.

2. Turn sharp right and the path descends to a fork. Take the right-hand path, which continues steeply down to a gate and stone stile in the bottom right-hand corner of the field. Climb the stile, keep ahead beside Humbleton Burn on the left to a lane, cross over and walk along the left edge of a car park and picnic area. Cross a footbridge over the burn and at a St Cuthbert's Way post, turn left and head uphill through trees to a gate at the top. Go

8. Battle of Homildon Hill 1402

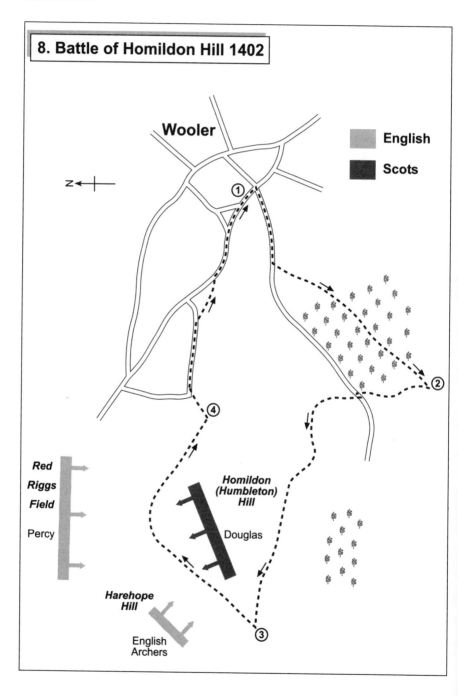

Wooler

English

Scots

z

① ②

④

Red
Riggs
Field

Percy

Homildon
(Humbleton)
Hill

Douglas

Harehope
Hill

English
Archers

③

through, keep ahead across open moorland, go through another gate and at a footpath post in front, turn left along a track. At a fork, take the right-hand track which curves right and continues uphill to a gate. Go through and continue across the glorious heathery moorland, looking out for a footpath post.

3. Turn right – here leaving St Cuthbert's Way – onto a path which descends through the gap between Humbleton Hill on the right and Harehope Hill to the left. Douglas and the Scottish army occupied Humbleton (Homildon) Hill, obviously a highly advantageous position for launching a battle. But the deadly attack of the English archers stationed on the opposite Harehope Hill forced the Scots from the hilltop down on to the lower ground. It was in the fields seen ahead – on the other side of the A697 and then called Red Riggs – that the bulk of the English army was drawn up and where most of the killing took place.

Climb a stile, continue downhill and at the bottom, the path bends right to continue below the slopes of Humbleton Hill. Climb two more stiles and eventually go through a gate onto a track.

4. Turn left, go through a gate, keep ahead to a junction and turn right along a lane. Where the lane curves left, turn right at a public footpath sign to Burnhouse Road, and go through a kissing gate. Walk along the left edge of a field and continue between bushes to another kissing gate. Go through and keep ahead across the next field, descending to go through a kissing gate in the right-hand corner. Turn right along the road into Wooler and continue down High Street to the Market Place.

What else is there to see?

The Bendor Stone, which commemorates the battle, can be seen in a field on the north side of the A697 about 2 miles (3.2km) north west of Wooler. It occupies the site of Red Riggs, the heart of the battle and scene of the greatest slaughter.

9

Battle of Hedgeley Moor, 25 April 1464

An absence of public footpaths in the area makes it virtually impossible to devise a longer route than this, at least not without considerable road walking. However, the walk does take you across the heart of the battlefield, passes the main surviving physical reminders of the battle and, as a bonus, there are striking views of the Cheviots on the skyline.

Start: Hedgeley Moor Battle Site, on A697 about 5½ miles (8.9km) south east of Wooler, grid ref NU050198

Distance: 2½ miles (4km)

Time: 1 hour

Parking: Layby on A697 beside battle site almost opposite entrance to a sawmill

Refreshments: None

Map: OS Explorer 332 (Alnwick & Amble)

The Battle

Unlike the vast majority of battles in this guide, this one and the battle of Hexham the following month were not fought between English and Scots but were Wars of the Roses conflicts between Lancastrians and Yorkists. Both parties were fighting for the throne of England.

Despite recent Yorkist victories at the battles of Mortimer's Cross and Towton in 1461, and the accession of the Duke of York to the throne as Edward IV in the same year, there was still considerable Lancastrian resistance in the north of England. This was mainly organised by Queen Margaret, the formidable consort of the deposed

The Percy Cross on the site of the battle

Henry VI, and Sir Ralph Percy. Percy raised a small army in Northumberland, assisted by Lord Hungerford and Lord Roos. This prompted a Yorkist army commanded by Lord Montagu, the younger brother of the Earl of Warwick, to march north to Newcastle. After acquiring reinforcements at Newcastle, Montagu continued northwards and confronted the Lancastrians at Hedgeley Moor to the south-east of Wooler.

The Lancastrians appear to have been taken by surprise and both Hungerford and Roos, realising that they were outnumbered, took the view that discretion was the better of valour and retreated southwards to Hexham. Sir Ralph Percy, however, was made of sterner stuff and he and his men remained to do battle with the enemy. Percy led a charge, making straight for Montagu in an attempt to kill the enemy leader. During this charge his horse is alleged to have made a huge leap – and the traditional spot where this is supposed to have happened can be seen today – but Percy was killed shortly afterwards.

Not surprisingly, Lancastrian resistance crumbled after the death of their leader and the Yorkists gained a relatively easy victory. The loss of such a powerful leader as Percy was a major blow to the Lancastrian cause in the north.

The Route

1. There are information boards in the enclosure beside the lay-by; the two boulders are alleged to represent the huge leap made by Sir Ralph Percy's horse during the battle before its master was killed. The enclosure is situated roughly where the Lancastrian army was drawn up at the start of the conflict across both sides of the present A697. The Yorkists were about a quarter of a mile (0.4km) to the south.

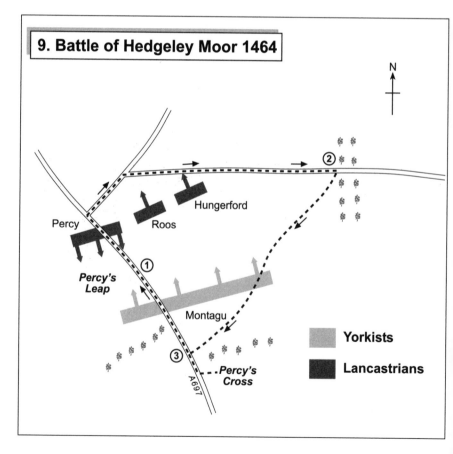

9. Battle of Hedgeley Moor 1464

N

Hungerford

Percy

Roos

Percy's
Leap

①

Montagu

②

③

A697

Percy's
Cross

Yorkists

Lancastrians

Begin by walking northwards along the main road and turn right along the road signposted to Eglingham and Alnwick. The road curves right and you keep along it for about 1 mile (1.6km).

2. At a public footpath sign to Percy's Cross and Fox Covert, turn sharp right through a gate. The field paths between here and the A697 take you across the heart of the battle site and there are views of the Cheviots on the skyline. Walk diagonally across a field, heading down into a shallow dip and then up again, and look out for a gap in a fence where there is a yellow waymark. Go through this gap, continue in the same direction across the next field towards a circle of trees, veer left, picking up a grassy track, and head gently downhill to go through a gate. Keep ahead by a fence on the left and where the fence bears slightly left, bear right and continue across the field to the far right corner. Just to the right of the corner, climb a waymarked stile and keep ahead, between the spoil heaps of the sawmill on the right and a stream on the left, to another stile. Climb that and ascend steps onto the A697.

3. The starting point is just under half a mile (0.8km) to the right, taking you through both the Yorkist and Lancastrian lines. Before doing that, a brief detour to the left, turning left through a gate and walking through a belt of trees, brings you to Percy's Cross, a monument to the battle.

10

Battle of Hexham, 15 May 1464

There is some dispute as to the exact site of this small encounter but a combination of public footpaths and lanes takes you around the likeliest area of fighting. This is a most attractive, undulating walk, much of it through or above the valley of Devil's Water, and there are fine views over the surrounding hilly and well-wooded countryside just to the south of Hexham and the Tyne valley.

Start: Opposite Hollybush Nursery and Sawmill on the B6306 about 2½ miles (4km) south east of Hexham and ½ mile (0.8km) south of Linnels Bridge, grid ref NY959611

Distance: 6 miles (9.7km)

Time: 3 hours

Parking: Layby almost opposite Hollybush Nursery, but do not park in front of the gate

Refreshments: None

Map: OS Explorer OL 43 (Hadrian's Wall)

The Battle

The battle of Hexham was really a follow-up to the battle of Hedgeley Moor, fought less than a month before. After leaving the Lancastrian army under Sir Ralph Percy in the lurch at Hedgeley Moor, Lord Hungerford and Lord Roos moved south to Hexham and joined up with another Lancastrian leader, the Duke of Somerset. The Yorkist leader, Lord Montagu, the Earl of Warwick's younger brother, set off in pursuit of them in order to complete the rout of the Lancastrians in the north.

Most of the fighting took place near Linnels Bridge in the valley of Devil's Water

On 14 May, Somerset camped a few miles to the south east of Hexham on the south bank of a stream called Devil's Water. The Yorkist army caught up with him on the following day and Montagu deployed his troops a short distance to the south of the Lancastrian position. The military engagement that followed was more of a skirmish than a battle. The Yorkists, who heavily outnumbered the Lancastrians, charged forward and trapped the Lancastrians against the stream. Lancastrian resistance collapsed and Somerset's men fled across the stream in confusion.

The triumphant Yorkists pursued them towards Hexham and many were killed in the retreat. Somerset was captured and later executed at Hexham; Hungerford and Roos suffered the same fate at Newcastle. For the time being, the Lancastrian cause in the north was at an end.

The Route

1. Facing the entrance to the nursery, turn right along the road. The Yorkists were drawn up to the left. In the 15th century the ground

would not have been covered by conifer woodland but was likely to have been open moorland. From here, the Yorkists charged down the slopes towards the Lancastrian position in the steep-sided valley of Devil's Water.

At a public footpath sign to Ordley, turn right along a tarmac drive and at a fork by a house, take the right-hand track, passing to the right of the house. By a barn on the left, look out for a waymarked post, which directs you to descend steps. Walk along a path to a stile, climb it and keep ahead near the top left edge of steeply sloping woodland, climbing another stile and continuing to join another path. Bear right along it, descending and turning left to cross a footbridge over Devil's Water. Climb steps and the way continues through Nunsbrough Wood to emerge onto a track.

Turn right, continue uphill through woodland and look out for a waymarked post where you bear left off the track onto a narrow downhill path. Cross a footbridge, continue across attractive meadowland beside Devil's Water, climb a stile and keep ahead along an enclosed track, still by the stream. The track becomes a lane, which heads up to a crossroads.

2. Keep ahead and at a public footpath sign to Newbiggin, turn right along an enclosed track. In front of the gates of a bungalow, turn left to go through a gate, turn right by a wall on the right and bear left to go through another gate. Continue by the right edge of the next three fields and in the third field, descend steeply to where you have a choice between a stile or gate. Having exercised that choice, turn left across a field, picking up the right edge and continuing along it to a gate.

Go through, keep ahead, climb a stile and bear left across the next field making for the far corner. Just before reaching it, join a tarmac track, climb a stile and continue towards farm buildings. Look out for where you climb the next stile, walk along a narrow path by a fence on the left, climb another stile and keep ahead to a road.

3. Turn left downhill, cross a bridge and at a fork about 100 yards

10. Battle of Hexham 1464

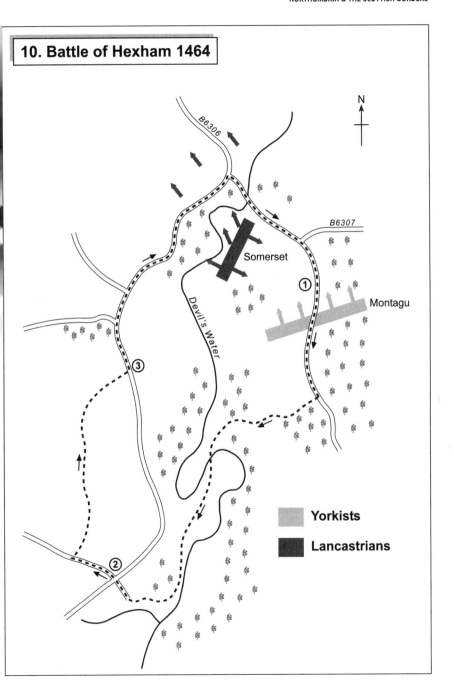

(91m) beyond, take the right-hand, uphill, narrow lane. Follow this winding lane to a T-junction and turn right downhill to cross the narrow Linnels Bridge over Devil's Water.

The area around this bridge was where the main conflict took place. The Lancastrians were on the south side of Devil's Water and their Yorkist opponents, advancing on them from near the starting point of the walk, engaged Somerset's men in hand-to-hand fighting and drove them across the stream. It is easy to appreciate how fighting in such hilly terrain must have been both hazardous and confusing, especially for the outnumbered Lancastrians.

Follow the road uphill to return to the start.

11

Battle of Flodden, 9 September 1513

This is arguably the most evocative and certainly the most informative and accessible battle site in Northumbria and the Scottish Borders. Its location provides the atmosphere: a battle monument that overlooks a now tranquil landscape of empty rolling hills, magnificent and extensive views and few sounds apart from birdsong and the rustling of the wind. The information and access comes from a Battlefield Trail, which forms part of the route and takes you across the heart of the battle site along lanes, permissive paths and public footpaths punctuated by information boards. As the walk heads first over Branxton Hill and then onto Flodden Edge, there is some climbing and expect a few overgrown stretches on some of the cross-field paths.

Start: Flodden Field Battle Site, signposted from A697, half a mile (0.8km) west of Branxton, grid ref NT888374

Distance: 7 miles (11.3km)

Time: 3½ hours

Parking: Flodden Field Battle Site car park

Refreshments: Pub at Crookham

Map: OS Explorer 339 (Kelso, Coldstream & Lower Tweed Valley)

The Battle

The background to the Battle of Flodden was the usual scenario in the saga of Anglo-Scottish warfare. England invaded France, the

French king requested help from his Scottish ally and the Scots obliged by invading northern England.

On this occasion, it was Henry VIII who went to war with France. The French king Louis XII invoked the 'Auld Alliance' and in 1513 James IV of Scotland, Henry's brother-in-law, invaded England. In the absence of the king, the English army was led by Thomas Howard, Earl of Surrey, over 70 years old but an able and highly experienced warrior. He marched north into Northumberland and at Alnwick he was joined by his son, Lord Thomas Howard, who he appointed his second-in-command.

Meanwhile James IV awaited the arrival of the English army from the south and placed his army in a formidable position on Flodden Edge, over 500 feet (152m) high and protected by steep slopes and marshy ground at the bottom. Realising that this was not a good position in which to hold a battle, Surrey decided to outflank the enemy. He divided his army and continued his march northwards, passing to the east of the Scots and then swinging round to cross the River Till. The English now lay between the Scottish army and the border and James was forced to move his army around and reposition it about 1¼ miles (2km) further north on the ridge of the marginally lower Branxton Hill. James's caution at being unwilling to withdraw from an invulnerable hilltop position caused the Scots to miss a good opportunity to attack the English while their army was divided. Instead, they watched as Surrey deployed his men on the slopes of Piper's Hill just to the south of the small village of Branxton.

The Scots had a bigger army, estimated at over 30,000 and considered to be the largest and best equipped Scottish force ever to cross the border into England. The English numbered around 26,000. After an initial artillery duel, in which the English came off better, a charge by the Scottish left, led by Lord Home, smashed its way through Howard's men and inflicted heavy casualties. Thinking that the English were more or less defeated, James was tempted to leave his hilltop position and charged down the hill at the English army into the boggy ground in the dip between the two hills. Slowed down by the terrain, the Scottish advance was held by Surrey's troops and in the bitter hand-to-hand fighting that followed, the English infantry were the more disciplined and effective.

The Battle Stone overlooks the scene of the fiercest fighting

Now came two decisive contributions. First the English reserve cavalry, led by Lord Dacre, came to Howard's aid and drove off Home's troops on the Scottish left flank. Secondly Sir Edward Stanley's rearguard force advanced from the east up the slopes of Pace Hill and attacked the Scottish right flank. So devastating was the onslaught by Stanley's archers that the Scots fled down the hill in terror and confusion. By now, the battle was virtually over and although the Scots fought bravely, the death of James IV inevitably had a profound effect.

In little over two hours the Scottish king, a substantial proportion of the Scottish nobility and three bishops lay dead on the battlefield. Scottish losses were heavy – around 10,000 – while the English army only lost about 4,000. It was one of the most decisive of English victories. Howard's reward from a grateful king was to be reinstated in his dukedom of Norfolk, which had been taken from him by Henry VII as a result of siding with Richard III in the Battle of Bosworth.

The Route

1. From the car park take the path signed Battlefield Trail. Climb steps and turn left for a brief detour to the monument. The simple but dignified monument stands on Piper's Hill where the English army was drawn up. Immediately ahead is the dip below Branxton Hill, which was the scene of most of the fighting and the heavy Scottish losses.

    Return to the path, continue uphill along the right edge of a field and in the top corner, cross a footbridge and go through a gate. Turn left along the left edge of two fields and go through a gate onto a lane. It is near to this spot that James IV is alleged to have been killed. Turn right, continue uphill over Branxton Hill and, where the lane bends left, is where the Scottish army was deployed at the start of the battle. The lane later curves right and continues over the ridge of the hill. At a T-junction, turn right.

2. Take the first lane on the left, signposted to Milfield and Wooler, which climbs gently and curves left onto Flodden Edge, giving a magnificent view of the Cheviots to the right. At a public footpath sign to Blinkbonny, turn left over a stile and walk across a field to climb another stile on the far side. The wooded ridge to the right was the site of the original Scottish position before James IV was outflanked by the English and forced to turn round and move further north. Bear left downhill across the next field, climb a stile and turn left along the left field edge to climb another stile. Bear right diagonally across the next field to emerge onto a track at the end of a belt of trees. Cross the track and keep in the same direction across a field towards farm buildings. In the far corner, go through a gate onto a lane and turn right.

3. At a public footpath sign to Crookham, turn left through a gate and walk along an enclosed track. Where the track bends right just in front of some trees, keep ahead along the right edge of the trees over the shoulder of two low hills. To the left are the slopes of Pace Hill up which Stanley's archers advanced to attack the Scots on Branxton Hill. At the end of the trees, continue by a fence on the

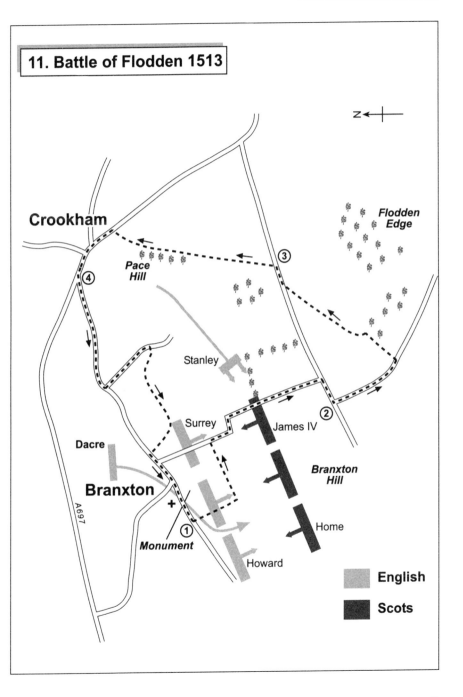

11. Battle of Flodden 1513

Crookham

Flodden
Edge

Pace
Hill

Stanley

Surrey

Dacre

Branxton

James IV

Branxton
Hill

Home

A 697

Monument

Howard

English

Scots

left. Go through two gates to emerge onto the A697 on the edge of Crookham and turn left.

4. In front of the Blue Bell Inn, turn left along a lane signposted to Branxton and Flodden Field Battle Site. Take the first lane on the left (signposted to Mardon) and head uphill. At the top, just in front of farm buildings, turn right along a track and immediately turn right again through a gate, at a public footpath sign to Branxton. Descend steeply into a dip, passing to the right of a line of sheds, head uphill and climb two stiles in quick succession to enter a conifer plantation. Continue through the trees, climb a stile on the far side and keep ahead along the right edge of the next two fields.

About half-way along the edge of the second field, look out for where a yellow waymark directs you to turn right through a gate. Walk diagonally across a field and go through a gate on the far side just to the right of the field corner. Keep along the left edge of a garden, descend steps and continue beside a house to emerge onto a lane in Branxton. Turn left through the village and at a fork, take the left-hand lane, signposted to Flodden Field, passing Branxton church. The present building is mainly Victorian but it was to its medieval predecessor that many of the bodies – both English and Scottish – were brought after the carnage of the battle. Continue along the lane to the start.

What else is there to see?

There are displays and further information on the battle at Etal Castle, about 4 miles (6.4km) away.

12

Battle of Solway Moss, 24 November 1542

The battle was fought in the heart of the 'Debatable Lands', the territory between the Eden and Esk bordering the Solway and fought over for centuries by English and Scottish kings. Apart from the buildings of Longtown on the northern edge of the battlefield and the planting of some woodland, there have been few changes in this area since the time of the battle. The walk encircles the site and because of the largely flat and open terrain, gives fine views across it, especially from the higher points, plus more extensive vistas across the Solway marshes and Esk valley to the line of the Southern Uplands of Scotland.

Start: Longtown, crossroads in town centre (junction of English Street, High Street, Swan Street and Esk Street), grid ref NY379687

Distance: 5 miles (8km)

Time: 2 hours

Parking: Roadside parking in Longtown

Refreshments: Pubs and cafés at Longtown

Map: OS Explorer 315 (Carlisle)

The Battle

After the death of James IV at Flodden, the new Scottish king, James V, was a seventeen month old baby. During his long minority and as a result of the heavy losses at Flodden, Scotland was relatively weak and posed no great danger to England. But when the

The predecessor of Arthuret church near the English-Scottish border overlooked the Battle of Solway Moss

new Scottish king reached maturity, close relations were re-established between France and Scotland, a situation that infuriated Henry VIII who had attempted to forge an alliance with his northern neighbour and nephew.

In 1542, Henry sent an English army across the border on a raiding expedition. There was much slaughter and destruction and, in retaliation, James V sent a Scottish army across the River Esk into England. A small English force under Sir Thomas Wharton marched out of Carlisle to intercept it.

The two armies met on the flat marshy land bordering the Solway between the rivers Esk and Lyne. It was all over quickly. Although the English were outnumbered, Wharton advanced and to his surprise Scottish resistance crumbled. A decisive factor was that the Scots had no leader. James had not accompanied his army into England, presumably thinking his presence was not necessary, and incredibly had failed to appoint a deputy.

Although it was more of a skirmish than a battle, the result was a crushing blow both to James and his country. As the Scots retreated back to the border, many were drowned in the rivers and marshes of Solway Moss and James himself died two weeks later. His successor was his six-day old daughter, Mary Queen of Scots, thus condemning a weak Scotland to another long minority.

The Walk

1. From the crossroads, walk along Esk Street and where the road peters out, keep ahead beside a gate and continue along a track. The track later keeps beside the River Esk, the border between England and Scotland. After passing beside a gate, you reach a fork. Take the left-hand track, which veers away from the river and continues on top of an embankment above a series of pools on the right. At a wire fence in front, bear right to keep beside it, go through a gate and keep ahead to the river again.

    Turn sharp left along a track which bears left, cross a footbridge over a beck and continue along the track to a gate. Go through, walk along a hedge-lined tarmac track and follow it around first a right and then a left bend towards a farm. The track bends right and left again between the farm buildings to emerge onto a lane.

2. Turn left, cross a bridge over a disused railway line and take the first road on the right. There is a wooded hill on the left and over to the right superb views over the site of the battle. Follow the road to a crossroads and cross the A7. Around here was where some of the fiercest fighting took place. Take the lane opposite, signposted to Brisco Hill, which bends left to reach the A6071.

3. Turn left – there are verges – and opposite a lane on the right (and just after a bridge), turn left over a ladder stile, at a public footpath sign to Fauld Mill Bridge. Walk along an embankment, above a field on the right and a beck on the left, climb a stile and continue along the left edge of a field. Where the beck bends sharply left, keep ahead – a line of widely spaced trees indicate the old hedgeline – making for a public footpath sign where you climb a stile onto the A7 again.

    Cross over and climb the stile opposite. Bear right across a field,

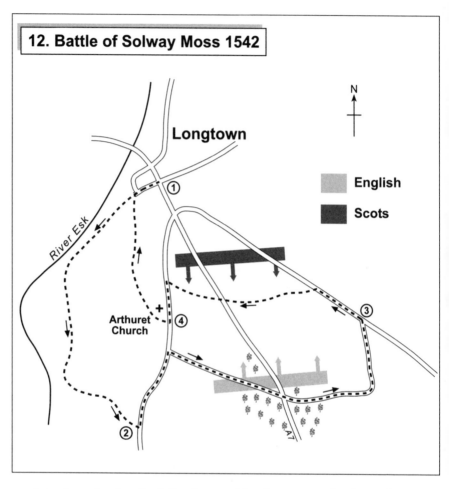

12. Battle of Solway Moss 1542

Longtown

N

English

Scots

River Esk

Arthuret
Church

A7

later keeping by the left edge, and in the corner climb a stile onto a road. Turn left towards St Michael's Church at Arthuret, a name which indicates that this area has connections with the legendary King Arthur.

4. At a public footpath sign to Longtown via St Michael's Well, turn right through a kissing gate into the churchyard of St Michael's Church, situated approximately where the Scots lined up at the start of the battle. It was its predecessor that witnessed the fighting; the present church is an early 17th-century rebuilding. As you

walk across the churchyard, there are more grand views across the Solway and Esk valley to the line of the Southern Uplands. For the remainder of the route, you are following more or less in the footsteps of the defeated Scots as they tried to make their way back across the River Esk into Scotland.

Go through a kissing gate on the far side and turn right along an embankment by a hedge bordering the churchyard. At a hedge corner, keep ahead to go through a kissing gate and steps on the left lead down to St Michael's Well, enclosed by railings. Keep ahead to go through another kissing gate, bear left off the embankment and head down to a footbridge over a ditch. Cross it, turn right alongside the ditch and at a footpath post, bear left across the field to the next footpath post where you cross a footbridge over a beck. Keep ahead and climb a stile in the field corner. Walk along the left edge of the next field, climb a stile onto a road and turn right to return to the start.

13

Destruction of Kelso Abbey and Roxburgh Castle, 1540s

The ruins of the once-wealthy Kelso Abbey and the remains of the once-great castle of Roxburgh are scarcely 1½ miles (2.4km) apart but their fates, and the fact that so little survives of either building, illustrate much about the troubled history of the Borders. This mainly 'there and back' walk leads from the centre of the handsome town of Kelso, along the banks of the rivers Tweed and Teviot, to the mound that is all that is left of the mighty castle and a flourishing town that gave its name to a Scottish county.

Start: Kelso, The Square, grid ref NT727339

Distance: 4 miles (6.4km)

Time: 2 hours

Parking: Kelso

Refreshments: Pubs and cafés at Kelso

Map: OS Explorer 339 (Kelso, Coldstream & Lower Tweed Valley)

Kelso Abbey and Roxburgh Castle 1540s

The accession of the infant Mary to the Scottish throne gave Henry VIII another opportunity to forge an alliance with his troublesome northern neighbour. He suggested a marriage between Mary and his son Edward – soon to become Edward VI – but the Scots rejected the offer, preferring to continue with their traditional alliance with France.

The impressive west end is all that remains of Kelso Abbey, the greatest of the Border Abbeys before the destruction of the 1540s

Henry was not a man to take rejection lightly. Furious at the close ties between Scotland and France, a source of great danger to England, he ordered Edward Seymour, Earl of Hertford and brother of Henry's third wife, Jane Seymour, to invade Scotland. Large English armies crossed the border in 1542, 1544 and again in 1545 with orders from the king to carry out wholesale burning and pillaging. The Scots described this policy of trying to arrange a marriage alliance by force as the 'rough wooing'. The Borders suffered particularly badly from this orgy of destruction and the great border abbeys – Kelso, Jedburgh, Melrose and Dryburgh – were among the principal victims.

The Tironensian abbey of Kelso was the largest and wealthiest of this collection of monasteries. It was founded by David I in 1128, just across the river from his royal castle at Roxburgh, and the building of it took just over a century. Its wealth came largely from the vast estates that it owned in the Cheviots and it witnessed the coronation of two Scottish kings, James III and James IV.

Proximity to the English border ensured that it was frequently the target of attacks during the many border raids of the 14th and 15th centuries. Hertford's invasions in the 1540s were particularly destructive and the abbey never recovered from the devastating raid in 1545. The eagerness of local people to make use of the ruins as a source of free building material, both here and at Roxburgh Castle, only hastened its decay.

A short distance away was the castle and town of Roxburgh, one of the major burghs of medieval Scotland. All that is left of it is the site of the castle marked by a large mound on the banks of the River Teviot. Roxburgh was at its height in the 12th and 13th centuries when – along with Edinburgh, Dunfermline and Berwick – it was one of the four most important burghs in Scotland. It had several churches and its own mint and was frequently the seat of the royal court. The trouble was that, being of strategic importance and close to the border, it was one of the principal objectives of English attacks, especially during and after the invasions of Edward I. Like nearby Berwick, it often changed hands between the two countries but was more frequently in the hands of the English.

During the long period of English occupation in the 14th and 15th centuries, the Scots repeatedly attacked and burnt the town of Roxburgh, inevitably accelerating its decline, but failed to capture the mighty castle, in its almost impregnable position above the Tweed and Teviot. It was finally taken after a siege in 1460 but at the cost of the life of James II. The Scottish king was killed through standing too close to a cannon when it exploded. The castle was then levelled to the ground in order to prevent its future use by the English.

That is not quite the end of the story because in the 1540s an earth and timber fort was built on the site by Hertford's invading armies but this idea was abandoned and the hastily constructed fort destroyed. By 1550, both Kelso Abbey and Roxburgh Castle had been largely reduced to rubble and the town of Roxburgh had totally disappeared.

The Route

1. The walk starts in The Square in front of Kelso's elegant town hall. Take the road to the right of it (Woodmarket), turn right and almost immediately turn left along The Butts. Follow the road

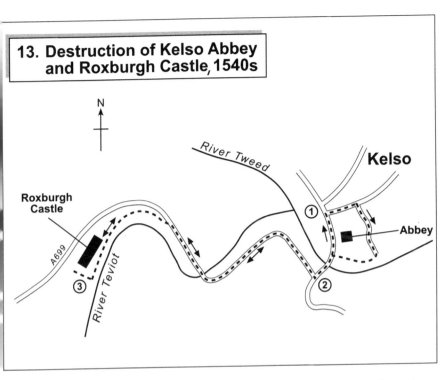

13. Destruction of Kelso Abbey and Roxburgh Castle, 1540s

around right and left bends and continue down to the River Tweed. Turn right along a tarmac riverside path, which curves right up to the road to the right of Kelso Bridge and turn left to cross the bridge. From here is a fine view of Floors Castle, a grand country house owned by the Duke of Roxburghe.

2. On the other side, turn right, in the St Boswells and Selkirk direction, and follow the Tweed up to its confluence with the Teviot. The road curves left to keep beside the Teviot and turns sharp right to cross a bridge over it. At a Borders Abbeys Way sign a short distance ahead, turn left over a stone stile and walk along a path above the river.

Descend steps and continue beside the river, following it around a left bend and below the scanty remains of Roxburgh Castle. Keep ahead as far as a stile and another stile on the right gives you access to the castle mound. Even without much of the masonry, the huge mound rising above the river is an impressive sight and it must have once been a formidable fortress. It is also a good view-point over both the Teviot and Tweed valleys and there is another particularly fine view of Floors Castle from the top of the mound.

3. Retrace your steps to Kelso Bridge and continue along the road, passing the abbey ruins, to the start. Although only part of the west end survives, it is a superb example of Norman architecture and enough to give some idea of the splendour of the abbey in its heyday.

14

Battle of Ancrum Moor, 27 February 1545

This 'there and back' walk takes you along part of the Roman road of Dere Street, the route used by the English army, to the site of the battle. There are fine views over the surrounding countryside, including striking views of the distinctive three peaks of the Eildon Hills.

Start: Junction of A68 and lane signposted to Maxton and Longnewton, about 6 miles (9.7km) north of Jedburgh and 1½ miles (2.4km) south of St Boswells, grid ref NT604291

Distance: 3 miles (4.8km)

Time: 1½ hours

Parking: Laybys near road junction

Refreshments: None

Map: OS Explorer OL16 (The Cheviot Hills)

The Battle

The battle of Ancrum Moor took place during the English invasion of 1545. It was part of Henry VIII's policy known as the 'rough wooing', an attempt to force the Scots to abandon their traditional alliance with France and agree to a marriage between the young Mary Queen of Scots and Prince Edward, heir to the English throne. The Earl of Hertford led the invading army and while he was further north pillaging St Andrews and Edinburgh, individual raiding parties were creating havoc and spreading destruction throughout the Borders.

In February 1545 one of these raiding parties led by two knights,

Lilliard's Grave overlooks the battlefield of Ancrum Moor

Sir Ralph Evers and Sir Brian Latoun, was returning to Jedburgh after plundering Melrose Abbey. A small Scottish army commanded by the Earl of Angus was waiting for it on Gersit Law, a hill about 5 miles (8km) north of Jedburgh which overlooks the old Roman road of Dere Street. The Roman road is almost certainly the route taken by the English but there is some difference of opinion as to the precise location of the battle. Some accounts place it a little further south on the slopes of Peniel Heugh, the distinctive peak that is now crowned by the Waterloo Monument. But Gersit Law, and the fields at its base seem the more likely location, and is the one that appears on Ordnance Survey maps.

Although they were outnumbered, the Scots used a clever tactic. Angus feigned a retreat and this tricked Evers and Latoun into believing either that a quick victory was in the offing or that they ought to attack now in case the Scots were going for reinforcements. Despite the fact that their men were tired from marching and laden down with booty, they charged up the hill but on reaching the top, the Scots fell upon them with great ferocity. The pikemen and spearmen were particularly effective and the English were pushed back. Pursued by the rampant Scots, the English retreated in panic down the hill and fled across Ancrum Moor. Both Evers and Latoun and around 800 of their men were killed in the rout; Scottish losses were light.

Although a small battle, it was a great triumph for the Scots and English armies were temporarily cleared out of Scotland. But two years later, despite the death of Henry VIII, they were back to continue the 'rough wooing', of the Queen of Scots.

The Route

1. Start by walking along the lane signposted to Maxton and almost immediately turn right, at a St Cuthbert's Way sign and Roman helmet symbol, onto a path through trees. As well as being part of St Cuthbert's Way, the path is on the line of the Roman road of Dere Street. This ran more or less along the line of the present A68 from Corbridge on Hadrian's Wall to the fort at Newstead near Melrose, hence the Roman helmet. This was also likely to be the route taken by the English army in 1545 while travelling between Melrose and Jedburgh.

   After crossing a bridge over a burn, the path turns first left and then right, continues between fences and heads up to a stile. Climb it, turn right and then almost immediately left to continue through woodland. On joining a clearer path, bear left along it to regain the line of the Roman road. Cross a footbridge and climb a stile to leave the trees. The way now continues along the right edge of several fields and over a series of stiles, finally continuing along an enclosed path to another stile. The hill seen over to the right, crowned by a Victorian mausoleum, is Gersit Law. This is where Angus and his army were camped and this is the hill up which the English disastrously charged in the hope of a quick victory.

   Climb the stile, keep ahead through trees once more and after crossing a footbridge, climb gently onto the top of Lilliard's Edge to Lilliard's Stone and Grave; the former is at the side of the path, the latter is accessible by a stile on the right.

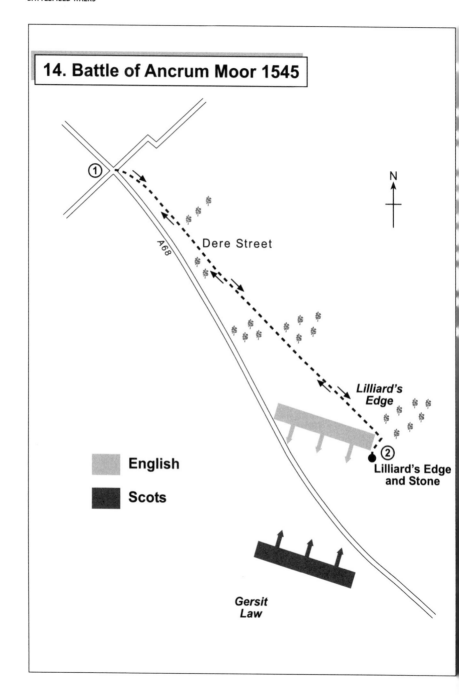

14. Battle of Ancrum Moor 1545

N

A68

Dere Street

Lilliard's
Edge

① Lilliard's Edge
and Stone

English

Scots

Gersit
Law

2. According to legend, Lilliard was a redoubtable woman whose lover had been killed by the English. To avenge his death, she fought in the battle with great tenacity and ferocity, hacking into the English and even continuing with the fight after her legs had been cut off. An inscription on the stone tells the story. The views from the edge are superb, ranging over the battlefield and across a wide expanse of the Borders and dominated by the three peaks of the Eildons.

From here, retrace your steps to the start.

15

Battle of Pinkie, 10 September 1547

Despite being in what is now a fairly built up area close to the eastern suburbs of Edinburgh, this is a surprisingly rural walk. An attractive path beside the River Esk takes you quickly from the town centre of Musselburgh into greener and quieter surroundings and much of the battle site is still open country. The views extend from Falside Hill, where the English army was camped, to the distinctive bulk of Arthur's Seat in Holyrood Park and along the coast to the Firth of Forth.

Start: Musselburgh, south side of bridge over the River Esk, grid ref NT343726

Distance: 6 miles (9.7km)

Time: 3 hours

Parking: Car parks in Musselburgh

Refreshments: Pubs and cafés at Musselburgh, pub at Whitecraig

Map: OS Explorer 351 (Dunbar & North Berwick)

The Battle

Henry VIII died in January 1547 and as his successor Edward VI was only nine years old, England like Scotland was governed for the time being by a regent. In England regency power was exercised by Edward Seymour, formerly Earl of Hertford and now Duke of Somerset, a veteran of campaigning in Scotland. He immediately continued Henry's policy of 'rough wooing'; trying to force a marriage between the young king of England and the even younger Queen of Scots. His Scottish counterpart was the Earl of Arran.

This medieval bridge at Musselburgh, controlled by the Scots, was the only crossing over the River Esk at the time of the Battle of Pinkie

Exasperated by the continuing close links between Scotland and France, Somerset invaded Scotland in September and advanced on Edinburgh. The English army was considerably reinforced by a large number of warships, which sailed towards the Firth of Forth under the command of Lord Clinton. Arran marched out from Edinburgh with a large army of over 25,000 and deployed his men on a ridge above the west bank of the River Esk. It was a virtually impregnable position, especially as he had a much larger army than his opponent and controlled the only bridge across the river. Somerset's army of around 17,000 men took up an equally strong position on Falside Hill above the eastern side of the river.

The day before the battle – 9th September – there was a brief and senseless skirmish between the rival cavalry troops, allegedly caused by the Scots taunting the English. It led to the destruction of much of the Scottish cavalry, a severe blow and a bad omen. Also, some of the English troops occupied a hill nearer the river close to Inveresk church, although there is some dispute as to whether they did this during the day before the battle or on the morning of the encounter. Somerset hoped to partially offset Arran's advantages by building a mound, now called Oliver's Mound, near the church and mounting some cannon on it.

On the morning of 10 September, the English moved down from Falside Hill and as Somerset advanced, he was amazed and no doubt relieved to see that the Scots had abandoned their strong position. Arran had already crossed over to the east side of the river and was advancing towards him. Impatience and perhaps an over-confidence caused by superior numbers may have led to this rash action but it proved to be disastrous.

An English cavalry charge led by Lord Grey failed against the stiff resistance of the Scottish pikemen. But heavy English artillery fire from Falside Hill, augmented by Clinton's warships firing on the Scots from just off Musselburgh in the Firth of Forth, had a devastating effect. The Scots were pushed back and fled with huge losses. It was a virtual massacre and many of those who managed to elude their English pursuers were drowned as they retreated across the River Esk.

It was one of Scotland's worst defeats and it has been estimated that over 10,000 of their soldiers were killed. English losses on the other hand were negligible. However, the English failed in their main objective as, not surprisingly, Somerset's 'rough wooing' did not achieve the desired result of a marriage alliance between England and Scotland. Instead, the young Mary Queen of Scots was shipped off to France and betrothed to the Dauphin.

The Route

1. Facing the bridge, turn left along the riverside path, passing the old bridge over the Esk. Despite being called the Roman Bridge, it is a medieval structure and was for many years the only bridge across the river. At the battle of Pinkie, it was controlled by the Scottish army and protected by artillery.

    After crossing a road and descending steps, the route continues along an attractive, tree-lined, tarmac path beside the Esk and the surroundings soon become more rural. Pass first under a railway bridge, and later under the A1, and the path eventually rises up to a road.

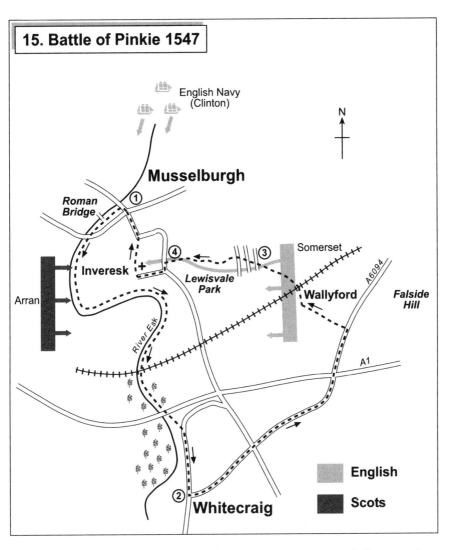

15. Battle of Pinkie 1547

English Navy
(Clinton)

N

Musselburgh

Roman Bridge ①

Inveresk ④

Lewisvale Park

③ Somerset

Arran

River Esk

Wallyford

A6094

Falside Hill

A1

② **Whitecraig**

English

Scots

2. Turn right into Whitecraig and at a T-junction, turn left. Just after crossing the bridge over the A1 – by a cycleway turning on the left – you pass a battle stone. The bulk of the battle was fought in the fields on both sides of this road and over to the right is Falside Hill where Somerset's army was camped. The occupants of Falside Castle, which can be seen on the ridge, barricaded themselves in and fired on the English army. In revenge, Somerset is alleged to

have set fire to it after the battle. To the left, there is a view of the coast and the Firth of Forth. English ships, commanded by Clinton, were anchored off the coast and artillery fire from them had a decisive effect on the outcome of the battle, although it is doubtful how far they could come up the narrow and shallow River Esk.

Keep ahead towards the houses of Wallyford but, before reaching them, turn left along a tarmac track, at a public footpath sign to Pinkie and Musselburgh. Over to the left is a view of Arthur's Seat, the prominent and distinctive hill that reaches down almost into the city centre of Edinburgh. Soon a path bears off to the right around the side of a sewage works building, goes under a railway bridge and continues – later becoming pleasantly tree-lined – to a road.

3. The next part of the walk is through a housing estate. Keep ahead along Pinkie Drive, turn right at a T-junction and take the first road on the left, Edenhall Crescent. Where the road curves left, keep ahead along a tarmac path, keeping roughly in a straight line and crossing several roads. After crossing the last of these roads (Park Lane), the route continues by a line of trees on the right through Lewisvale Park. At a footpath sign, a brief detour to the left up a winding path brings you to a plaque in a wall which records that Somerset camped on this ridge on 9 September, the night before the battle.

    Continue through the park to emerge onto a road.

4. Turn left uphill and at the top, turn right along a road to Inveresk church. The present church was built in 1805 but its predecessor was in the thick of the fighting in 1547. Somerset built a mound for his cannon nearby which a century later was used by Oliver Cromwell for the same purpose, hence its name Oliver's Mound.

    Turn right into the churchyard, pass to the left of the church and descend steps. Continue along a broad, walled tarmac track to a road and turn right. The first road on the left (Dalrymple Loan) leads back to the start.

16

Battle of Newburn Ford, 28 August 1640

The walk encircles the part of the battlefield that lies on the
north bank of the River Tyne and takes you up onto Heddon
Law. It was from here that the Scots overlooked the English
army camped on the meadows on the south side of the river.
Considering that this area is now within the suburbs of
Newcastle and was previously heavily industrialised with coal
mines in the vicinity, it is remarkably open with virtually
uninterrupted views over the site of the battle.
Twentieth-century industrial decline and the subsequent
conversion of much of the battlefield into a green and pleasant
riverside park have undoubtedly helped.

Start: Newburn, Tyne Riverside Country Park next to Newburn
Leisure Centre, grid ref NZ161656

Distance: 6½ miles (10.5km)

Time: 3 hours

Parking: Tyne Riverside Country Park

Refreshments: Pubs at Newburn, pub and tea room at
Heddon-on-the-Wall

Map: OS Explorer 316 (Newcastle upon Tyne)

The Battle

Charles I wanted religious uniformity throughout both his kingdoms and in 1637 attempted to force the Church of England
prayer book on the largely Presbyterian Scots. The Scots resisted and
in 1638 signed a Covenant, pledging to reject the prayer book and to
abolish bishops in Scotland. The result was the outbreak of two short

The Scots mounted cannon on the church tower at Newburn prior to the battle

wars between Charles and the Scottish Covenanters in 1639 and 1640, known as the Bishops' Wars. The Battle of Newburn Ford took place during the second of these.

A Scottish army of around 20,000 men, led by the very able Alexander Leslie, invaded England and marched on Newcastle. Leslie was intending to cross the Tyne at Newburn – just to the west of Newcastle where there were two fords across the river – and attack the city from the south. Lord Conway, who was in charge of strengthening the defences of Newcastle at the time, scrambled together an army of around 5,000 and hastily erected two sconces (defensive earthworks) on the south bank of the river opposite Newburn. Conway positioned his artillery on the sconces and intended a holding operation here, while awaiting the arrival of reinforcements from York.

On the evening of 27 August, the Scots were at Heddon Law on the north bank of the river overlooking the English position. During the night, Leslie mounted light cannon on the tower of Newburn church and his soldiers moved down into the village. The following day the two armies nervously eyed each other up for several hours until the shooting – possibly accidental – of a Scottish soldier started the battle. The Scots attacked and the cannon in the church tower proved extremely effective, inflicting great damage on the English earthwork defences. A constant artillery onslaught by the Scots led to heavy casualties amongst the English soldiers and by 4 pm – one of the few times in the day when the river was fordable – the Scots were able to force their way across the Tyne. Despite dogged resistance from the English cavalry, ably led by Lord Wilmot, the Scots were triumphant and the English fled in panic.

Both Newcastle and Durham subsequently surrendered to the Scottish army. Leslie did not return to Scotland until August 1641 and then only after the payment of a bribe of £200,000 to free Newcastle. The Scottish success in the Bishops' Wars had a direct bearing on the outbreak of the Civil War in England in 1642. It was his acute shortage of money, largely caused by these wars, that forced a reluctant Charles I to recall Parliament in 1640. Many of the members of this Parliament – the famous Long Parliament – were in a belligerent and furious mood and were determined to seize this great opportunity to curtail the power of the king.

The Route

1. Exit from the car park, cross the road and at a public bridleway sign, walk along a path parallel to the road – initially by a hedge on the right and later the hedge is on the left – into Newburn village. On reaching a road just to the left of Newburn Bridge, turn left for a brief detour to Newburn church. Turn left again at a T-junction, take the first road on the right and turn right at the next T-junction to the church. It was in the Norman west tower of this church that the Scots mounted cannon on the evening before the battle (27 August), a tactic that was to play a decisive part in the ensuing battle.

    Retrace your steps to the bridge.

2. Turn right, not along your previous path but along a tarmac path and cycleway beside the River Tyne. This is part of the Hadrian's Wall Path, here called Hadrian's Way. The bridge did not exist in 1640 but it was near here that the Scots were able to ford the Tyne in order to attack the English on the south side of the river.

Changes in the river flow would make this virtually impossible to-day. The sconces that the English erected on the south bank as some form of defence have entirely disappeared.

Follow the regular Hadrian's Wall Path waymarks and acorn symbols for 2 miles (3.2km) beside the Tyne, passing the Country Park Visitor Centre. Eventually a waymarked post directs you to turn right away from the river to a gate.

3. Go through, turn left along a track and at a footpath sign to Heddon-on-the-Wall, turn right through a kissing gate and head in a straight line across a golf course. On the far side, continue uphill along a track through woodland. Follow the track around a left curve and immediately after going through a gate, turn sharp right and continue uphill. Pass beside a gate, keep ahead and the track curves right and later becomes a lane.

From these heights, you get an excellent view over the battlefield. It is similar to the view that Leslie had of the English position, and it was down these slopes that the Scottish army advanced on Conway's much smaller force. Continue uphill into Heddon-on-the-Wall and at a T-junction, turn right along Towne Gate.

4. Take the first turning on the right – here leaving Hadrian's Wall Path – and head downhill. Look out for a public footpath sign to Newburn and Bank Top where you turn left through a kissing gate and walk across a field. Go through another kissing gate and continue along a path through woodland. The path becomes enclosed and continues to a stile. Climb it, turn right along a track, take the first track on the left, pass beside a gate and keep ahead. Shortly after a right bend, turn left along a tree-lined track, which leads back to the start.

What else is there to see?

There is a display and leaflet on the battle of Newburn Ford in the Country Park Visitor Centre, passed near the start of the walk.

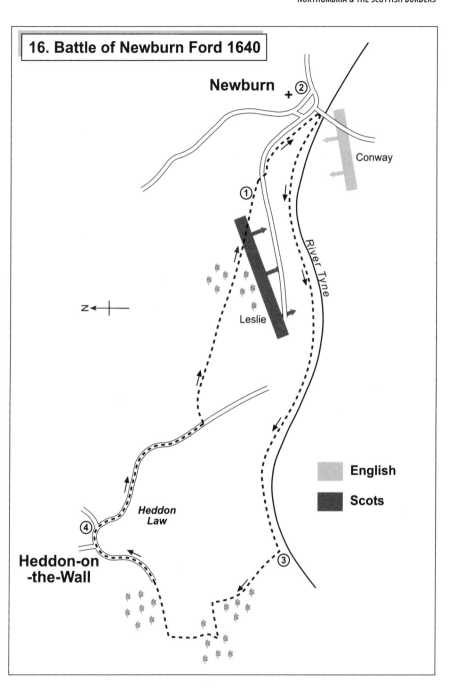

16. Battle of Newburn Ford 1640

Newburn

Conway

River Tyne

Leslie

Heddon Law

Heddon-on
-the-Wall

English

Scots

17

Battle of Philiphaugh, 13 September 1645

From the centre of Selkirk you head down into the valley of Ettrick Water, walk across the site of the battle and head up into the hills and woods of the Philiphaugh Estate on the other side of the valley. The views over the valley and the rolling hills of Ettrick Forest are magnificent, route finding is easy and the climbing is steady rather than strenuous.

Start: Selkirk, by the Town Hall, grid ref NT470285

Distance: 6½ miles (10.5km)

Time: 3½ hours

Parking: Selkirk

Refreshments: Pubs and cafés at Selkirk

Map: OS Explorer 338 (Galashiels, Selkirk & Melrose)

The Battle

The English Civil War was really a British Civil War as it obviously embraced Wales, dragged in Ireland and had profound consequences for Scotland. After all Charles I was king of Scotland as well as England and he had his supporters and opponents both north and south of the border. Philiphaugh was not the usual English v Scots conflict but was a Scottish battle fought on Scottish soil between two sets of Scots; Royalists (supporters of the king) and Covenanters (those who supported the Covenant of 1638 pledged to protect the Presbyterian religion).

In 1643, the Scottish Parliament decided to give military assis-

It was through the gap between Peat Law and Linglie Hill that the Covenanters advanced on the Royalists prior to the Battle of Philiphaugh

tance to the English Parliamentarians, on the assumption that a Parliamentary victory would be in the best interests of Scotland. Although previously a supporter of the Covenanters, James Graham, Marquis of Montrose, remained loyal to the king and became the main champion of the Royalist cause north of the border. In 1645, after a series of stunning victories against the Covenanters, Charles I ordered him to march south to the Borders.

On 12 September Montrose arrived at Philiphaugh near Selkirk. Here he camped in a secure position at the junction of the Ettrick and Yarrow rivers, protected by the two rivers to the south and the hills of Ettrick Forest to the north. Meanwhile David Leslie, commander of the Scottish forces fighting in England, marched back into Scotland. By 12 September, unknown to Montrose, he was camped nearby between Selkirk and Galashiels. Leslie had around 6,000 men; Montrose only had around 700 as many of his Highland and Irish troops had gone back home and his recruiting efforts in the predominantly Presbyterian Borders had received a lukewarm response.

Next morning Leslie advanced towards Philiphaugh and split his army into two groups. One group, led by Agnew of Lochnaw, moved northwards through the gap between Linglie Hill and Peat Law and attacked Montrose's troops from the rear. Leslie commanded the second group, which marched along the river valley. Taken by surprise and hopelessly outnumbered, Montrose's men stood little chance. Hastily dug trenches proved inadequate and although Montrose led a spirited cavalry charge against Leslie's horsemen and fought bravely, his troops were driven back with huge losses.

The lucky ones, including Montrose himself, escaped over Minch Moor. The Irish troops that surrendered were either massacred on the battlefield or while in captivity at nearby Newark Castle. For the moment the Royalist cause was over in Scotland as well as in England.

The Route

1. Begin by heading steeply downhill along the winding A707 and cross Selkirk Bridge over Ettrick Water. The battle was mostly fought in the fields between the river and the A708, part of which is now occupied by Selkirk Rugby Club. Take the second road on the left and pass to the right of the rugby ground to reach the junction of the A707 and A708. Keep ahead along a lane, signposted Philiphaugh Walks, and follow it to a car park.

2. Turn left and take the uphill track that leads from the car park. For the next part of the walk up to a small reservoir you follow a yellow waymarked route and keep above Long Philip Burn on the left. At a fork, continue along the left-hand track by the bottom left edge of sloping woodland. The track later climbs steadily through woodland and at the next fork, take the right-hand uphill track which curves left and continues along the top right edge of the trees.

3. Just in front of a yellow waymarked post by a small reservoir, turn left to cross a footbridge over the burn and climb a stile. Keep ahead across grass to a fence corner, bear first right and then left and head steadily uphill along the right edge of a field. For the

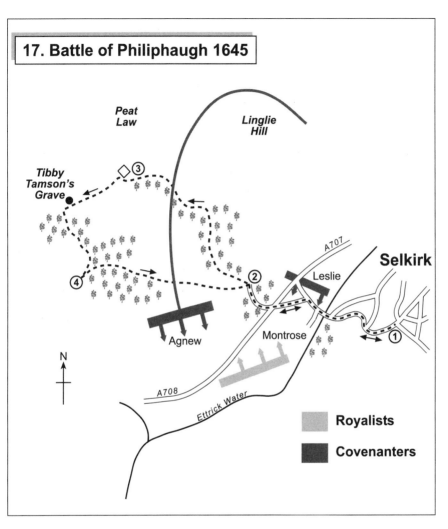

17. Battle of Philiphaugh 1645

next part of the route you follow red waymarked posts. To the right is a view of the pass between Linglie Hill and Peat Law down which the Covenanters marched to attack the Royalists in the rear. On the right – and accessible by a stile – you pass the grave of Tibby Tamson. She lies in this remote spot because she was accused of being a witch and therefore could not be buried in consecrated ground.

Keep ahead to climb a stile in the field corner and walk along the right edge of conifer woodland to the next waymarked post. Ahead is a grand view of Newark Castle where many Irish prisoners, fighting on the Royalist side, and their womenfolk were massacred by the victorious Covenanters after the battle. At the post turn left downhill through the trees, cross a track and keep ahead to a T-junction. Turn left and, at a fork, take the right-hand path which curves right to a gate. Go through, turn left along the left edge of a field and, in the corner, follow the edge to the right. In the next corner, go through a gate, walk along the left edge of the next field and again follow the edge to the right to keep by the right edge of woodland.

4. On reaching a track, turn sharp left over a stile and follow the track downhill through the trees. Keep ahead on the main track all the while and gaps in the trees reveal views over Selkirk and the battle site. The track eventually reaches a lane. Turn right and retrace your steps to Selkirk Bridge and on up the hill back to the start.

18

Battle of Dunbar, 3 September 1650

This is a 'there and back' walk as there is a virtual absence of public footpaths across or around the perimeter of the battlefield. Using a combination of roads, lanes and tracks, the route takes you up onto the slopes of Doon Hill, where the Scottish army was camped prior to the battle, which not only overlooks the battle site but gives you superb views over Dunbar and the East Lothian coast.

Start: Broxburn, on the A1087 about 200yards (183m) north of the bridge over the Brox Burn and about 1¼ miles (2km) south of Dunbar town centre, grid ref NT693774

Distance: 4 miles (6.4km)

Time: 2 hours

Parking: Layby at Broxburn on west side of A1087

Refreshments: None en route but pubs and cafés nearby in Dunbar

Map: OS Explorer 351 (Dunbar & North Berwick)

The Battle

The end of the Civil War in England came in 1646 with the surrender of the Royalist forces and the imprisonment of Charles I. Two years later in 1648 a Second Civil War broke out. This arose because the wartime alliance between Parliament and the Scots broke down and following secret negotiations with the king, the Scots switched sides and a Scottish army invaded England on his behalf. It was a brief affair: Cromwell defeated the Scots at Preston and they returned home.

The battle stone on the site of the Battle of Dunbar

It was largely this treachery that convinced Cromwell and other Parliamentary leaders that Charles I should be tried for high treason. The king's subsequent execution in January 1649 infuriated the Scots and they proclaimed his son King Charles II. The new king's aim was to win back his English throne, with the aid of a Scottish army and the support of English Royalists. This prompted Cromwell to make a pre-emptive strike and in 1650 he invaded Scotland with an army of around 16.000 and marched on Edinburgh. The city was defended by a large Scottish army of over 20,000, led by Cromwell's former ally David Leslie. Cromwell was forced to fall back on Dunbar but a rapid march by Leslie outflanked him and blocked his way southwards to the border.

Leslie positioned his troops on Doon Hill to the south of Dunbar which effectively trapped the English army. Cromwell urgently needed to get back to England. Winter was approaching, he was short of supplies and sickness had already reduced his army to around 11,000. But the only routes available were either to squeeze through the narrow coastal plain between Doon Hill and the sea – highly dangerous with the Scots positioned on Doon Hill – or to be rescued by the fleet and escape by sea. All Leslie needed to do was wait.

But Cromwell could hardly believe his luck when on 2 September, Leslie moved his troops from their hilltop position into the valley of the Brox Burn (or Spott Burn) in preparation for a battle. It is thought that he may have been pushed into this rash action by over-zealous clerics who believed that God was on their side. These religious fanatics had already dismissed some of the professional soldiers who were not considered 'godly 'enough. It was a monumental blunder. Cromwell now decided to take the fight to the enemy and prepared a surprise attack for early on the following morning. This attack by Lambert's cavalry troops and Monk's infantrymen took place before dawn. The Scots defended valiantly and held the English until a devastating cavalry charge later in the morning by Cromwell's New Model Army swept away Leslie's right wing. When Cromwell's men later swung round and attacked the remainder of the Scottish army from the rear, the rout was complete. The Scots fled from the battlefield and around 3,000 were killed and 10,000 captured.

Edinburgh was taken and Leslie retreated to Stirling. The final battle between him and Cromwell was to take place exactly a year later at Worcester. The outcome was the same and Charles II was forced to go into exile for the next nine years.

The Route

1. Start by walking southwards along the A1087 away from the sea and the road curves left to cross the Brox Burn. After the Scots moved down from their position on Doon Hill, the two armies were drawn up on either side of the small burn – also called the Spott Burn – and the bulk of the fighting took place in the open fields that are now bisected by the A1 and main east coast railway line.

    About half a mile (0.8km) further on you pass a battle stone and beyond that you cross a railway bridge to reach the A1.Turn left, cross carefully, take the first turning on the right, signposted 'Historic Scotland, Doon Hill', and head uphill along a lane.

18. Battle of Dunbar 1650

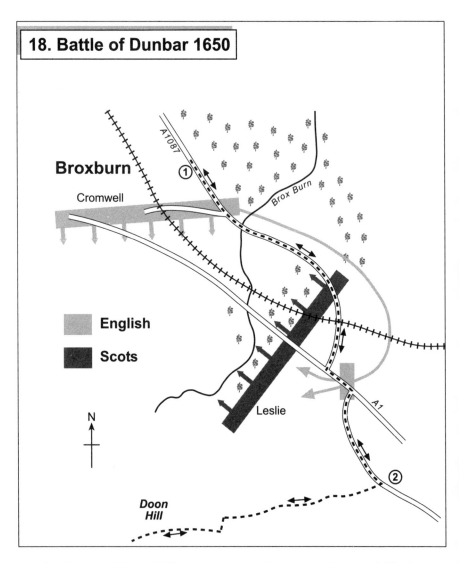

2. At the next Doon Hill sign, turn right to continue uphill along a narrow tarmac track. Just after a left bend, turn right onto a rough track. Ahead is the summit of Doon Hill and to the right are magnificent views over the battlefield to Dunbar and the coast. Go through a kissing gate, keep ahead and, where the track ends, a gate on the left admits you to a field. The field is the site of a Dark

Age settlement, comprising a burial site and a 7th-century Anglo-Saxon hall. .

It lies just below the top of the hill and is as far as you can go. From here retrace your steps downhill to the start, enjoying more grand views over Dunbar, the East Lothian coast and the site of the battle below.

What else is there to see?

There is information on the battle in the Town House Museum in Dunbar.

19

Battle of Prestonpans, 21 September 1745

From the battle viewpoint, itself a former coal tip, the view over the main battle site and towards the coast is dominated by a power station but there is little visible evidence now that this was once a coal mining area. The walk begins near the viewpoint, passes a monument to a local man killed in the battle and continues along a lane used as an escape route by some of the defeated Government army.

Start: Prestonpans, Meadowmill Sports Centre, follow Battle Site signs from B1361, grid ref NT402737

Distance: 3 miles (4.8km)

Time: 1½ hours

Parking: Meadowmill Sports Centre

Refreshments: None en route but there are pubs and cafés in Tranent town centre, a brief detour from the route

Map: OS Explorer 351 (Dunbar & North Berwick)

The Battle

Charles Edward Stuart, grandson of James II and commonly called 'Bonnie Prince Charlie', was known as the Young Pretender. In July 1745 he landed on the west coast of Scotland to claim the throne on behalf of his father, James Edward Stuart, the Old Pretender. Since the passing of the Act of Settlement in 1701, the Stuarts had been barred from the British throne because they were Roman Catholics.

The way up to the viewpoint and information boards overlooking the site of the battle

The throne was occupied at the time by the Hanoverian king, George II.

Despite a slow start – some Highland chiefs were reluctant to support him – the clans flocked to his cause and by the middle of September Charles and his supporters, called Jacobites, had captured Edinburgh virtually unopposed. Britain was at war with France at the time and most of the army was overseas. Government forces in Scotland only numbered around 3,000 at the time and they were under the command of Sir John Cope. In order to crush the Jacobite uprising, Cope landed at Dunbar with his army and moved towards the Scottish capital. Although the government forces were largely inexperienced, they did have the advantage of greater numbers and superior weapons. The Jacobite army was totally lacking in artillery.

Cope deployed his troops near Preston House. It was a favourable position, less than 1 mile (1.6km) from the sea and protected on the south by the marshes of Tranent meadows. The Jacobites, led by Lord George Murray, occupied Falside Hill from where they overlooked their opponents. Realising that it would be unwise to charge at Cope across the marshland, Murray outflanked the government forces by leading his men along a little-known path – suggested by a local man – to the south of them and then swinging around to the east of Tranent in order to attack their weaker eastern flank. Cope had to reposition his troops quickly, not an easy manoeuvre.

The Jacobites charged and, overwhelmed by the ferocity of the attack, especially from the Highland clans, the government forces retreated in terror and confusion. The greater flexibility and mobility of the Jacobites, compared with the cumbersome and slow moving government troops, more than compensated for their smaller numbers and less sophisticated weapons. The battle was over so quickly that Cope's artillery scarcely had time for one volley before fleeing.

Although it was a relatively small battle, government losses were heavy compared with those of their opponents. Around 500 of Cope's men were killed whereas the Jacobites only lost about 40-50. Bonnie Prince Charlie and his supporters were now in a position to contemplate an invasion of England and a march on London.

The Route

1. Take the tarmac path which leads off from the car park through trees to the base of the battlefield viewpoint. This has been landscaped from a former coal tip, and provides not only a good view of the battle site but also a series of information panels. The battle took place mainly in the meadows immediately in front, between the viewpoint and the coast and either side of the B6371. The Jacobites had skilfully outflanked their opponents and were positioned to the east of the road.

   After climbing to the top, descend to continue along the tarmac path. Where it bends right to cross the railway line, keep ahead along a track. This is a winding track but it keeps more or less parallel to the railway. The tower seen ahead is Preston Tower, a 15th-century tower house near where Cope's government troops were positioned. The meadows to the left, now used as playing fields, were marshland at the time of the battle and Cope was hoping that they would offer him some protection. Later the route passes the monument to Colonel Gardiner, killed in the battle,

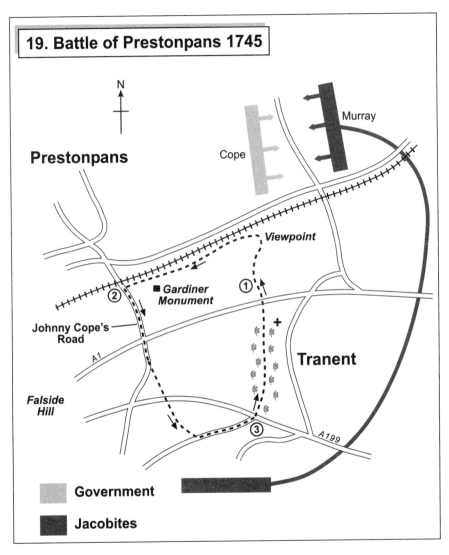

19. Battle of Prestonpans 1745

N

Prestonpans

Cope

Murray

Viewpoint

■ *Gardiner Monument*

① ②

Johnny Cope's Road

A1

Tranent

+

Falside Hill

③

A199

Government

Jacobites

and from the monument there is a fine view of his home, Bankton House.

2. On descending steps to a lane, turn left uphill, passing Bankton House. This lane is nicknamed Johnny Cope's Road, as it was along here that Cope and some of his men tried to escape after

their defeat. Cross a bridge over the A1 and, where the lane bends right, keep ahead up steps, at a public path sign, continue uphill along a path and climb steps onto a road. Take the path opposite and turn left along a broad track. The track becomes a road which leads into Tranent. On reaching a T-junction turn right.

3. Almost immediately turn sharp left, at a bridleway sign, onto a tarmac track. This is a former railway track that runs through a wooded ravine on the edge of Tranent. The railway was built in the 19th century, mainly to transport coal.

Follow this track under a road bridge and beside a barrier to a junction of paths just below Tranent church. The present church dates from 1800 but its 15th-century predecessor overlooked the battle site. Keep ahead, in the 'Viewpoint and Sports Centre' direction, and just after passing under the A1, turn left back into the sports centre car park.

What else is there to see?

There is a battle stone near the turning off the B1361 to the Sports Centre car park

20

Bonnie Prince Charlie at Carlisle, 1745

The sieges of Carlisle in 1745 – there were two, one by Bonnie Prince Charlie and the other by his adversary the Duke of Cumberland – were just the last of a long succession of sieges of this vulnerable and highly strategic border city and many of them have left their scars on Carlisle's buildings and fabric. The walk, which takes in most of Carlisle's historic buildings, including the castle, cathedral and remains of the medieval walls, clearly illustrates its troubled and often violent history.

Start: Carlisle, the Cross, grid ref NY402559

Distance: 2½ miles (4km)

Time: 1½ hours

Parking: Carlisle

Refreshments: Plenty of pubs, restaurants and cafés at Carlisle

Map: OS Explorer 315 (Carlisle) or town map of Carlisle

Carlisle, 1745

Throughout its long history, Carlisle changed hands many times between England and Scotland – though not as many as Berwick – and suffered a number of sieges. One such occasion was during the Civil War when Parliament's Scottish allies besieged it from October 1644 to June 1645. After the surrender of the Royalist garrison, mainly through starvation, the cathedral was ransacked and partially demolished.

The last siege of Carlisle – and indeed of any English town – was in 1745. After the Jacobite victory at Prestonpans the way was clear for Bonnie Prince Charlie's forces to invade England. The choice was to

The town hall – now tourist information and visitor centre – at Carlisle, scene of Bonnie Prince Charlie's proclamation of his father as King James III in 1745

take either the eastern route via Newcastle or the western route via Carlisle: On the advice of Lord George Murray, Charles decided on the latter. He left Edinburgh on 3 November, crossed the River Esk at Longtown – the border – on 8 November and marched on Carlisle. At the time the city's defences were weak and there was only a small garrison. Charles demanded the surrender of Carlisle on 10 November and the city capitulated four days later, a surrender described by General Wade as 'scandalous and shameful, if not treacherous'.

Charles himself entered the city on 17 November and proclaimed his father as King James III from Carlisle Cross. Between 18 and 20 November the Jacobites left the city to continue their march through north west England to London. They reached as far south as Derby and then decided to turn back, largely because of the dangers of penetrating further south with larger government forces ahead. By 19 December the Jacobites were back in Carlisle. Leaving a small garrison there, Charles and the bulk of his army recrossed the Esk on 20 December and returned to Scotland.

Meanwhile the Duke of Cumberland, who had been in hot pursuit of the Jacobites throughout their retreat from Derby, arrived outside the walls of Carlisle the following day. He commenced bombarding the city on 28 December and the small Jacobite garrison surrendered to him on 30 December.

Over 400 prisoners were taken and many were imprisoned in the cathedral before execution or transportation. Cumberland later continued his pursuit across the border and the decisive and final encounter took place at Culloden in April 1746. This, the last battle to be fought on British soil, marked the end of the Jacobite cause and the conclusion of centuries of Anglo-Scottish warfare.

The Route

1. Start at the Cross in front of the Town Hall (the latter now a tourist information and visitor centre), the traditional centre of the city. It was here that Bonnie Prince Charlie proclaimed his father King James III on 17 November 1745. Walk down English Street away from the Cross and turn left into Bank Street. On the wall of the Marks and Spencer store opposite Bank Street, two plaques indicate that both rival commanders, Bonnie Prince Charlie and the Duke of Cumberland, stayed in a former building on the site, Highmore House, in 1745.

   At a crossroads, turn right along Lowther Street to the twin drum towers of the Citadel. The Citadel was built by Henry VIII to strengthen this part of Carlisle's defences and rebuilt in the early 19th century to serve as law courts, the Court Houses.

2. Turn right between the two Court Houses back up English Street, turn left along Victoria Viaduct and turn right along West Walls. Later the road runs along the top of the only remaining stretch of Carlisle's medieval walls. Opposite steps on the left, turn right into Dean Tait's Lane and go under an arch.

3. The route continues to the left along Abbey Street but if you turn right under another arch you enter the cathedral precincts. No building in Carlisle wears its battle scars more openly than the cathedral. Immediately obvious is its unusual truncated appear-

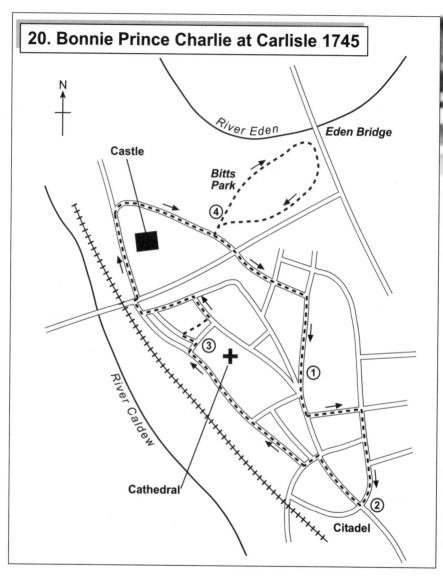

20. Bonnie Prince Charlie at Carlisle 1745

ance, the result of the demolition of most of the nave during the Civil War in order to repair the city's defences. Further damage was done in 1745 when it was used as a Jacobite prison. The cathedral was founded in 1133 but the east end had to be rebuilt following a fire in 1292. Its chief glories are the 14th-century choir and magnificent east window.

After turning left into Abbey Street, turn right, at a signpost to Castle, into the gardens of Tullie House Museum and Art Gallery, bending left and right and going under an arch into Castle Street. Turn left towards the castle, turn left again, parallel to the dual carriageway, and cross a footbridge over it to the castle. On the other side, pass under the footbridge just crossed and turn right beside a short stretch of the city walls. Either follow the road as it curves right around the base of the castle or walk along a path above the road which keeps beside the castle walls and then descends to join the road.

Carlisle Castle, one of the major border strongholds, was originally founded by William II in 1092 but has been restored and enlarged several times over succeeding centuries. The dominating feature is the massive 12th-century keep. Visitors are shown the 'licking stones', where in 1745 desperate Jacobite prisoners allegedly licked moisture from the stones in order to stay alive.

4. At this point you can make a brief detour to the Eden Bridge by turning left through a car park to enter Bitts Park. Walk along a broad tarmac path to a crossways, bear slightly right and keep above the River Eden to the bridge. This was – and still is – the chief route into Carlisle from Scotland. In front of the bridge, turn right and the path curves right along the edge of the park to return to the park entrance and the road (point 4 on map).

5. Turn left onto a path parallel to the road which passes under the dual carriageway and continue along West Tower Street, passing in front of the Market Hall. In front of Debenhams, turn right into Scotch Street to return to the Cross.

What else is there to see?

There is a display on the events of 1745 in Carlisle in the Tullie House Museum.

21

Battle of Clifton Moor, 18 December 1745

A combination of public footpaths and lanes enables you to encircle the battlefield and although the site is crossed by the M6, A6 and main London to Glasgow railway line, it remains surprisingly open and unspoilt. At many points, fine views extend across fields and moorland to the line of the Pennines on the east and the Lakeland mountains to the west.

Start: Clifton, north end of village by the church, grid ref NY534266

Distance: 4 miles (6.4km)

Time: 2 hours

Parking: Roadside parking by Clifton church

Refreshments: Pubs at Clifton

Map: OS Explorer OL5 (The English Lakes – North Eastern area)

The Battle

The encounter between the Jacobite army and government forces at Clifton Moor was really a series of skirmishes rather than a battle. It took place during Bonnie Prince Charlie's return march from Derby to Scotland.

The Jacobites left Derby on 6 December and on the difficult journey northwards they were pursued by government troops led by the Duke of Cumberland, one of George II's sons. Charles and the bulk of the Jacobite army arrived in Penrith on 18 December and learnt – by interrogating a member of the local militia – that Cumberland was

Clifton Tower, all that remains of a 15th-century manor house, overlooked the battle in 1745

closer behind than expected, approaching the village of Clifton just a few miles to the south. Lord George Murray marched to Clifton with three of the Jacobite regiments and lay in wait for Cumberland's forces behind the walls that enclosed some of the small fields around the village.

Conditions for fighting could hardly have been worse. It was a cold and snowy day and Cumberland's troops did not arrive until the late afternoon. Three of Cumberland's regiments were ordered to attack but, as they advanced across Clifton Moor towards the Jacobites, it was difficult to tell friend from foe in the gloom of a December evening. In the confused and fierce hand-to-hand fighting that followed, the Jacobites came off best and the government forces retreated across the moor.

Casualties were light on both sides but it was a moral victory for Murray. Both armies were exhausted by the combination of a long and rapid march and bad weather but Cumberland's men were halted in their tracks. This enabled Murray to rejoin the rest of the Jacobite army in Penrith and Bonnie Prince Charlie was able to slip back into Scotland unmolested.

The Route

1. Begin by walking southwards along the main road through the village and at a public bridleway sign about 200yards (183m) after crossing a railway bridge, turn left along an enclosed track. The route from here to the lane at reference point 2 would have been in the thick of the fighting.

    Recross the railway and keep ahead along the track, which bends right. After going through a gate, the track curves left to another gate. Do not go through it but turn left along the left field edge and head downhill to go through a gate in the corner. The route now continues more or less in a straight line – sometimes along the left edge of fields and sometimes along enclosed paths – before bending right to ford a beck. Again, you keep in a fairly straight line along field edges – with one stretch of hedge-lined track – finally going through a gate onto a lane.

2. Turn right, ignore the first lane on the right but turn along the second one. Cross a railway bridge, keep ahead to the A6, cross over and go through the gate opposite. Walk along a track to the left of farm buildings, go through a gate, bear left to go through another one and cross a bridge over the M6.

3. The track bears right and continues in a straight line. The heart of the battlefield is over to the right and at one point, a gap in the hedge reveals a view of two standing stones. After going through a gate, keep ahead across a field and look out for where you turn right over a stile. Walk diagonally across the next field, heading towards woodland on the left and, in the far-left corner, keep ahead along a track to a gate. Go through and continue along the track which bends left to run alongside the motorway.

    Go through a kissing gate, pass under a railway bridge and the track ascends gently to another kissing gate. Go through, turn right and recross the M6. Keep ahead along a track, passing to the right of Clifton Hall. All that remains of this 15th-century manor house is the tower, built around 1500. In 1745, it must have af-

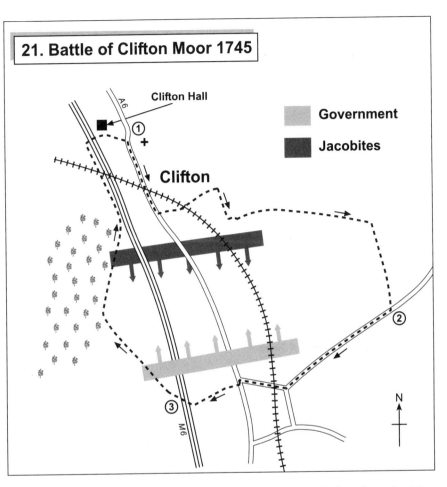

21. Battle of Clifton Moor 1745

Clifton Hall

Government

Jacobites

Clifton

N

forded a fine view of the battle, as indeed did the church. The track emerges onto the A6 opposite the church and starting point.

What else is there to see?

At the south end of Clifton almost opposite the George and Dragon, there is a seat and metal grille commemorating the battle.

22

German raid on Hartlepool, 16 December 1914

The walk starts by a surviving gun battery that was used to defend Hartlepool during the brief German attack in December 1914. A pleasant and invigorating stroll along the promenade is followed by a visit to the superb 13th-century church of St Hilda and a walk by a stretch of Hartlepool's medieval wall, built to deter earlier aggressors.

Start: Hartlepool, The Headland, by the Heugh Gun Battery, grid ref NZ534338

Distance: 3 miles (4.8km)

Time: 1½ hours

Parking: Car park by the Heugh Battery

Refreshments: Pubs in Hartlepool

Map: OS Explorer 306 (Middlesbrough & Hartlepool) or town map of Hartlepool

Hartlepool, 1914

On the morning of 16 December 1914, the people of Hartlepool had a shock. They found themselves in the totally unexpected situation of being bombarded by three German battle cruisers, out in the North Sea. .

The raid was carried out by a scouting group from the German fleet led by Admiral Franz von Hipper and the targets were the ports of Scarborough, Whitby and Hartlepool. It started at approximately 8.10

This plaque, by the Heugh Gun Battery, commemorates the German raid on Hartlepool in 1914

and lasted until around 9.30. The Germans unleashed 1,150 shells and there were around 130 killed and nearly 600 injured.

Two of Hartlepool's four coastal batteries, Heugh Battery and Lighthouse Battery, retaliated by firing 143 shells at the German warships, damaging three of them. Around 80 German sailors were killed and 217 injured.

The fact that the German navy could penetrate within firing range of Britain's coastline caused outrage and anger, not just in Hartlepool and the other two attacked towns, but throughout the whole of Britain. The country had not experienced an attack of any kind since the Napoleonic Wars over a century ago. Throughout the Victorian period, the British people had felt safe and secure in their island fortress, protected by the world's largest and most powerful navy. Public opinion condemned the raid as inhuman as the Germans were attacking defenceless civilians, an indication of how the British people on their seemingly invulnerable island had rather lost touch with the reality of modern warfare. The Germans justified it on the grounds that the ports were legitimate targets.

The German motive seems to have been to entice the British Grand

Fleet out of its anchorage at Scapa Flow in the Orkneys in order to engage it in battle. The Royal Navy had received intelligence reports of the German raiding force and sent out a detachment to intercept Hipper but a combination of confusion and inefficiency allowed Hipper both to slip through and carry out the raid and to subsequently escape. In Germany, he and his men were feted as heroes and the operation hailed as a great success.

In fact it was not a success and neither side could cover themselves with any glory. The German raid had no military value and had failed in its main objective to lure the British fleet out of harbour. Such an attack was never repeated but it could be regarded as something of a propaganda coup for the Germans and a shock to British morale. It was certainly a shock to many of the inhabitants of Hartlepool.

The Route

1. Some form of coastal defence had existed in Hartlepool since the building of the medieval wall in the 14th century. The first batteries were put up in the 1650s and were rebuilt or modernised at regular intervals until the construction of the present batteries. Building of these began in the 1860s as part of the fortifications ordered by Lord Palmerston in anticipation of a possible French invasion. Heugh Gun Battery was the first of these. It was built in 1860, rebuilt in 1898 and decommissioned in 1958. Nothing remains of its sister battery, the Lighthouse Battery, also built in 1860. A plaque on the wall of the battery records the events of December 1914.

    Begin by walking down to the sea and turn left along the broad promenade. Follow it by the rocky shoreline and above fine sandy beaches and where it ends, turn left up to a road.

2. Turn left along it (Marine Drive) parallel to your outward route. The road later veers right away from the sea and continues along the right edge of a grassy area, part of the former Town Moor, originally used for the grazing of animals. The beacon was erected in 1988 to commemorate the 300th anniversary of the defeat of the Spanish Armada. Keep ahead to reach a crossroads by St Hilda's

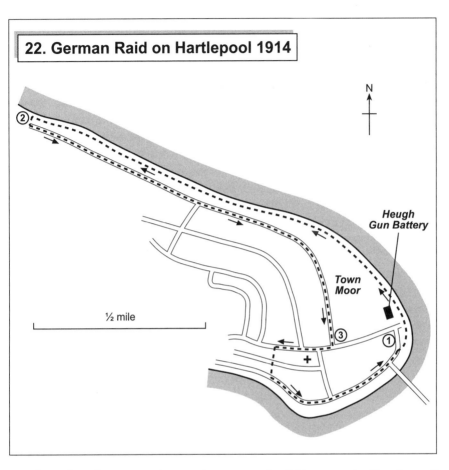

22. German Raid on Hartlepool 1914

church. This imposing 13ᵗʰ-century building, an indication of Hartlepool's wealth and importance in the Middle Ages, occupies part of the site of an Anglo-Saxon monastery.

3. Turn right into Church Close, passing to the right of the church. After following the road around a right bend, immediately turn left and at a footpath sign, turn left across a paved landscaped area. Cross a road (High Street) and keep ahead to a T-junction in front of Sandwell Gate and a surviving stretch of Hartlepool's medieval wall. The wall was constructed in the 14ᵗʰ century following a Scottish raid on the port in 1316.

Turn left alongside the wall, curving left and returning to the start along the promenade.

What else is there to see?

There is a display on the German raid of December 1914 in the Museum of Hartlepool.

Also of Interest

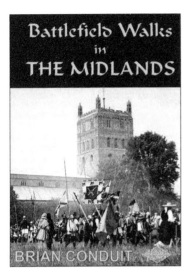

BATTLEFIELD WALKS IN THE MIDLANDS

Brian Conduit

Imagine the scenes in these 22 battlefield walks, featuring military engagements throughout the Midlands. There are 14 battlefields, 3 siege sites and the scenes of 5 other military events ranging from Charles II's escape from his pursuers at Boscobel House, to the World War II bombing of Coventry. Introductory material provides a summary of both the War of the Roses and the Civil War

Most of the sites are in peaceful and tranquil surroundings and situated amidst attractive countryside. Many have features of interest nearby - a ruined castle, a cathedral, an ancient house, or old churches and abbeys - to add to the interest and enjoyment of the walk. *£7.95*

BATTLEFIELD WALKS IN YORKSHIRE

David Clark

For historians, Yorkshire is of particular significance as it contains more important battlefields than any other English county, encompassing over one thousand years of history.

An opportunity to be transported back in time with these detailed accounts of historical Yorkshire battles sure to captivate the mind of any walker. Surrender to the invitation to discover historic sites of 23 famous battles between 633 and 1945. Enjoy 23 excellent walks in captivating scenery, each one including up-to-date information on access and facilities available in this beautiful region. *£6.95*

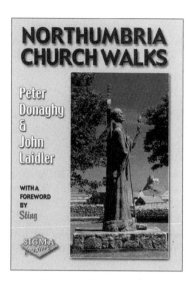

NORTHUMBRIA CHURCH WALKS
Peter Donaghy & John Laidler

International rock star, conservationist and Northumbrian **Sting** writes in the foreword to this book how he has so often found solutions to life's problems on long, solitary walks in this unspoilt part of England. The 30 walks range from 4 to 12 miles, each starting from a noteworthy church. With links between historical and cultural details of churches included with each walk, there are also easy-to-follow instructions combined with cross-referenced maps making this ideal both for those who wish to complete the full walk or those who prefer to visit the church and have a short stroll. *£8.95*

NORTHUMBRIA WALKS WITH CHILDREN
Stephen Rickerby

Covering the North East from the Tees to the Tweed, this guide book includes over 20 walks suitable for families. There are questions and spotting checklists to interest the children, as well as practical information for parents. All less than 5 miles long, the walks explore the great variety of scenery and heritage of Northumbria. As the parent of a young child himself, the author knows how to make sure kids don't get bored! *£6.95*

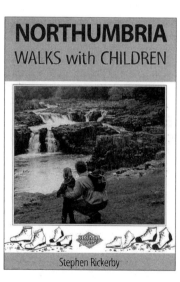

WALKING THE CHEVIOTS
Edward Baker

This is one of the few guides to a true wilderness area, written by an experienced author who has lived in the Cheviots all his life. Nearly 50 walks, from 2 to 14 miles. "This book is a must for the Cheviot walker, whether experienced in the area or a visitor eager to explore this unique range of northern hills." – RAMBLING TODAY *£8.95*

All of our books are available through booksellers, and online from Amazon.co.uk. In case of difficulty, or for a free catalogue, please contact:
SIGMA LEISURE, 1 SOUTH OAK LANE, WILMSLOW, CHESHIRE SK9 6AR.
Phone: 01625-531035   **E-mail:** info@sigmapress.co.uk
Web site (with current information on all Sigma titles): www.sigmapress.co.uk